BALANCED ASSESSMENT

FROM Formative TO Summative

Kay Burke

Solution Tree | Press a division of
Solution Tree

555 North Morton Street
Bloomington, IN 47404

800.733.6786 (toll free) / 812.336.7700
FAX: 812.336.7790

email: info@solution-tree.com
solution-tree.com

Printed in the United States of America

14 13 12 11 10   2 3 4 5

Excerpts from Georgia Performance Standards reprinted with permission from the Georgia Department of Education. © 2010 Georgia Department of Education. All rights reserved.

FSC
Mixed Sources
Product group from well-managed
forests and other controlled sources

Cert no. SW-COC-002283
www.fsc.org
© 1996 Forest Stewardship Council

Library of Congress Cataloging-in-Publication Data

Burke, Kay.

  Balanced assessment : from formative to summative / Kay Burke.

      p. cm.

  Includes bibliographical references and index.

  ISBN 978-1-934009-52-9 (perfect bound) -- ISBN 978-1-935249-24-5 (library binding) 1. Educational evaluation--United States. 2. Education--Standards--United States. I. Title.

  LB2822.75.B88 2010

  371.26--dc22

                      2009051128

Solution Tree

Jeffrey C. Jones, CEO & President

Solution Tree Press

President: Douglas M. Rife

Publisher: Robert D. Clouse

Vice President of Production: Gretchen Knapp

Managing Production Editor: Caroline Wise

Senior Production Editor: Risë Koben

Proofreader: Rachel Rosolina

Text and Cover Designer: Orlando Angel

To Carol M. Brown—my sister and my friend

Acknowledgments

I would like to offer a very special thank you to the following district and school administrators, curriculum specialists, coaches, and teachers, who not only worked together on teams to develop creative assessments for their students but generously allowed me to share their work in this book:

Carrollton City Schools, Carrollton, Georgia

Erin McGinnis (director of school improvement and curriculum/instruction)

Carrollton Middle School (grades 4–5): Trent North (principal); Debbie Williams (formerly associate principal; currently associate principal of Carrollton Elementary School); and Marva Bell, Lori Higgs, LaKeia King, and Shanon Melson (teachers)

Carrollton Junior High School (grades 6–8): Todd Simpson (principal); John Megathlin, Kisha Mitchell, Amy Mulvehill, and Camille Sanders (language arts teachers); and Patti Allen and Matilda Strickland (math teachers)

Clarke County School District, Athens, Georgia

Noris Price (associate superintendent of instruction), Mark Tavernier (director of the Office of Teaching and Learning), Veronica Jackson (administrative assistant), Kate Arnold (elementary math content specialist), Julie Bower (social studies content specialist), Claude Gonzalez (science content specialist), Glenda Huff (secondary math content specialist), and Barbara Michalove (elementary language arts content specialist)

Third-grade "Desk Dilemma" math unit: Kate Arnold (elementary math content specialist); Daphne Hall and Lisa Stanzi (elementary instructional coaches); and Lisa Lane (teacher)

Fourth-grade "Wanted: Snack Thief!" math unit: Molly Efland, Laura Forehand, and Brian Madej (elementary instructional coaches); and Joyce Moeller and Jenna Starnes (teachers)

Fourth-grade "H_2O: Where Did You Go?" science unit: Barbara Michalove (elementary language arts content specialist); Scherry Lewis and Claire Smith (elementary instructional coaches); and Carrie Bette-Duncan and Halley Page (teachers)

Fifth-grade "Fun With Fractions!" math unit: Louise Brockinton, Susan Cardin, and Kerstin Long (elementary instructional coaches); and Julie Hinkle and Leah York (teachers)

Fifth-grade "Changes in the Nye-ght" science unit: Karen Higginbotham (gifted specialist); Jan Miller-Burkins and Hallie Williamson (elementary instructional coaches); and Bertha Troutman-Rambeau (teacher)

Cobb County School District, Marietta, Georgia

Nancy Larimer and Andrew Smith (professional learning supervisors); Tracy Boyles and Ashley Kirby (area lead teachers); and John Christian Cali (teacher)

College of William and Mary, Williamsburg, Virginia

Whitney Slough (student in the Foreign Language Instructional Planning course taught by Janet D. Parker, School of Education, spring 2009)

Coweta County School District, Newnan, Georgia

Evans Middle School (grades 6–8): Brenda Foyle and Sean Parker (math teachers)

DeKalb County School System, Decatur, Georgia

Champion Theme Middle School (grades 6–8): Yvonne Stroud (teacher)

I appreciate all the help of Susan Gray and Jodi Keller and thank them for their invaluable assistance. I would also like to thank Claudia Wheatley, education specialist; Douglas Rife, president; and Gretchen Knapp, vice president of production, at Solution Tree Press for their support and flexibility and for allowing me to work with Risë Koben, senior production editor. Risë's expertise, patience, and sense of humor have inspired me to become a better writer and person. On my summative rubric for editors, she scores an "Exceeds All Expectations."

Solution Tree Press would like to thank the following reviewers:

Lisa Almeida
Senior Professional Development Associate
The Leadership and Learning Center
Englewood, Colorado

Heidi Andrade
Associate Professor, Department of
  Educational and Counseling Psychology
University at Albany
State University of New York
Albany, New York

Victoria L. Bernhardt
Executive Director
Education for the Future
Chico, California

Joseph Schrock
Director of Assessment
Jackson Public Schools
Jackson, Mississippi

Harry G. Tuttle
Educational Consultant
Mattydale, New York

Nance S. Wilson
Assistant Professor, Department of Teaching
  and Learning Principles
University of Central Florida
Orlando, Florida

Visit **go.solution-tree.com/assessment**
to download selected figures and forms.

Table of Contents

About the Author

Kay Burke works with her colleagues at Kay Burke & Associates to present professional development workshops for teachers and administrators on standards-based teaching and learning, formative assessment, and classroom management. She received her undergraduate degree from Florida Atlantic University, her master's degree from the University of Central Florida, her educational specialist degree from Emory University, her PhD from Georgia State University, and her administration certification from the University of Georgia.

Kay served as an award-winning English teacher, department chairperson, dean of students, mentor, and administrator in Florida and Georgia for twenty years. She also was the director of the field-based master's program sponsored by the International Renewal Institute (IRI/SkyLight) and Saint Xavier University in Illinois. Since 1990, Kay has designed and conducted professional development workshops and presented at conferences of the National Staff Development Council, the Association for Supervision and Curriculum Development, the National Association of Secondary School Principals, the National Association of Elementary School Principals, Solution Tree, and the International Reading Association, as well as at international conferences in Canada and Australia.

Kay has written or edited thirteen books on standards-based learning, formative assessment, classroom management, student and professional portfolios, and mentoring. Her best-selling books include *How to Assess Authentic Learning* (5th ed.); *What to Do With the Kid Who . . .* ; *Developing Cooperation, Self-Discipline, and Responsibility in the Classroom* (3rd ed.); *The Portfolio Connection: Student Work Linked to Standards* (3rd ed.); and *From Standards to Rubrics in Six Steps: Tools for Assessing Student Learning, K–8*, which was a finalist for the Distinguished Achievement Award from the Association of Educational Publishers in 2007.

Introduction

In the United States, the passing of the No Child Left Behind legislation in 2001 set into motion an ever-increasing emphasis on high-stakes summative evaluations. State tests were created to determine whether students had achieved adequate yearly progress (AYP) and would be promoted to the next grade. It seemed like the periodic reform pendulum had swung in the direction of back-to-basics instruction and assessment geared toward measuring the knowledge and skills of millions of students in all grade levels and content areas. Professional development workshops focused on helping teachers prepare students for practice benchmark tests, interim assessments, short-cycle assessments, and end-of-quarter tests—all with an eye toward making sure students would be ready to take the high-stakes summative tests at the end of the year. The public and politicians wanted to use standardized tests—assessment *of* learning—as the ultimate yardstick of how teachers and school systems were doing.

Publishing companies not only provided many versions of the high-stakes tests used by each state but also produced and marketed the so-called formative assessment benchmark tests that could be given to students throughout the year to find out if they were prepared for the final test. Some educators argued that practice test booklets and benchmark tests published by testing companies should not be labeled "formative assessment." These critics believed that real formative assessments were created by classroom teachers and used to provide ongoing feedback to their students on a daily basis rather than just predict the end-of-year test scores.

Soon the backlash began, and another movement was launched. Assessment *for* learning became the new rallying cry and the mantra of "must-attend, must-buy, must-do" workshops, conferences, professional development books, and journal articles. Rarely have prepositions like *for* and *of* played such a critical role in the educational future of students. It was almost like a competition between the summative high-stakes testing advocates, who valued only the one big test, and the formative camp, who advocated not grading anything but just providing feedback.

Educators should realize, however, that assessment is not an either/or scenario. Both formative and summative assessments are necessary; moreover, they complement each other. The goal of this book is to show teachers how to integrate both formative and summative assessments seamlessly into their instruction. The research, rationale, strategies, and examples provided will help teachers develop their own repertoire of formative and summative assessments to monitor, grade, and make inferences about a student's ability to meet standards and curriculum goals. In addition, the exercises at the end of each chapter will guide teachers in reflecting about the practices discussed and in planning action steps to implement those practices in their own schools.

Chapter 1: "Standards-Based Instruction and Assessment: Begin With the End in Mind" explores the impact of standards on teaching, assessment, and learning. Typically, teachers are overwhelmed by the sheer number and complexity of state standards. If teams of teachers work together to select the "power standards" and focus on teaching them, they will achieve better results. This chapter shows teachers how they can "repack" the standards by sequencing the steps in the order they should be taught and adding some kid-friendly vocabulary. This process helps students to gradually learn the language of the standards (LOTS), allows them to achieve a deeper understanding of the concepts, and helps prepare them for high-stakes state tests.

Chapter 2: "The Balanced Assessment Model: When Formative Meets Summative" examines the distinct ways in which formative and summative assessments support teaching and learning. The purpose and timing of the assessment determine whether it is categorized as formative or summative. The purpose of formative assessment is to provide feedback on an ongoing basis to *improve* student learning. Many formative assessments created by teachers embed the language of the standards and focus on the things students need to know and be able to do. When students are unable to understand the standards, teachers use corrective interventions and differentiated learning strategies to meet their students' diverse needs. Formative assessments are not usually graded. The purpose of summative assessment is to make a final judgment to *prove* what the student has or has not learned. A summative assessment could be the same assessment that was given at an earlier point as a formative assessment, but since it is administered at the end of a learning segment, it is usually graded. Both types of assessment play integral roles in providing a more accurate portrait of each student learner.

Chapter 3: "Common Assessments: A Community of Assessors" looks at the collaborative approach to designing assessments and analyzing results. Teachers would be overwhelmed if they were required to create valid performance tasks, checklists, and rubrics for all the standards by themselves. The solution is to have grade-level or content-area teams meet to determine the power standards and then create common assessments for all students. Later, the members of this community of learners meet to examine student work, analyze data, and develop additional teaching interventions to target struggling students and challenge more advanced students. Teachers who use common assessments help ensure that the school and the district require the same degree of quality and consistency to maintain equity.

Chapter 4: "Performance Tasks: The Key to an Engaging Curriculum" examines how to motivate students while teaching the required curriculum. The curriculum in many schools and districts does not meet the needs of today's students. Some of the textbook or district curriculum units are rigorous, but teachers may need to create original, authentic performance tasks to show how the curriculum is also relevant and meaningful to their students. These performance tasks target multiple standards, encourage group and individual work, and motivate students to engage in their own learning. Lessons targeting basic skills and standardized test preparation can be incorporated into the performance-task framework. Students, however, need a *context* for why they are learning the information. Performance tasks provide the relevance and interaction all students need to take ownership of their own learning and to transfer skills from school to life.

Chapter 5: "Checklists: Progressions of Learning" discusses the use and benefits of checklists for students and teachers and explains how teachers can create them. Checklists developed from the language of the standards provide the scaffolding to help students organize their thoughts and complete a multistep project or performance. Students need a plan, and until they learn how to formulate a plan and monitor their own work, they may need a checklist. Checklists spell out progressions of learning to show students what they have to do and how they can do it better.

Checklists serve a dual role. In addition to providing a framework or roadmap to help students begin a task and complete each step of the instructional process, they function as an assessment tool that can yield specific and ongoing feedback throughout the instructional process. A standards-based checklist can be difficult to construct, but teachers can work together to create and use this valuable instructional and assessment tool.

Chapter 6: "Rubrics: All Roads Lead to the Standards" shares the importance of using rubrics to assess the quality of students' work and to determine whether students have met the standards. Rubrics or scoring guides became popular when educators in most states created performance standards for students to meet. Traditional assessments such as quizzes and tests measure content knowledge and some skills. But when students are asked to demonstrate their ability to apply knowledge and skills in an authentic learning situation, the evaluation must be criterion based. When students conduct an experiment, deliver a speech, or write a letter, they have to meet specific criteria, which are described in the indicators for the standards. The judgment of performances, projects, and portfolios can be subjective in nature, but rubrics provide descriptors for different levels of performance and assign ratings or scores for each criterion. While checklists can show that a student attempted to meet the criteria, rubrics address the specific expectations for quality work.

Chapter 7: "Formative Assessment Tools: Real Time and Real Fast" describes more informal assessment tools that can be used on an ongoing basis to check for student understanding. Checklists and rubrics can be challenging to create and time-consuming to use, but teachers can use some quick strategies to assess students in real time. Learning logs and processing strategies like the "thinking moment" or the "wraparound" help students reflect on their learning and self-assess their understanding of key ideas and important concepts. These tools allow students to process smaller chunks of information and to clarify their thinking before they become confused or frustrated. At the same time, they provide the teacher with oral and written feedback to gauge students' understanding on a minute-to-minute basis throughout the lesson. These informal formative assessments also help teachers determine when to differentiate their instruction in order to meet the diverse learning needs of their students.

Chapter 8: "Summative Assessment and Evaluation: The Last Judgment" goes into more detail about the uses of summative assessment, looks at the role of benchmark or interim testing, and explains the relationship between assessments and evaluation. *Evaluation* is the process of reviewing all the work produced by the student and placing a value on it. Summative assessments provide the last information teachers need to assign a final grade to individual students. In addition, the data from summative assessments are used to analyze the rigor of the standards, the effectiveness of instructional programs, the impact of teaching and learning strategies, and the quality of the textbooks in order to make improvements for the next year.

Assessment drives instruction, and every teacher needs to build a repertoire of both formative and summative assessment strategies to help all students learn. Not every strategy works with every student, so it is important to have a toolbox of differentiated assessments to meet the needs of all students. This book is intended to provide some useful tools for responding to the never-ending challenge of helping students to meet and exceed standards and to participate more fully and enthusiastically in their own learning.

1

Standards-Based Instruction and Assessment: Begin With the End in Mind

The idea of "beginning with the end in mind" means establishing goals for students to meet and then designing curriculum, instruction, and assessment around the desired outcomes. This is not a new idea, and there have been various attempts to put such an approach into practice.

What Are Behavioral Objectives?

In the 1960s, teachers struggled with having their students meet "behavioral objectives." Behavioral objectives were very specific, and they addressed discrete bits of knowledge and skill that could be measured precisely. Measurement expert Robert Mager's book *Preparing Instructional Objectives* (1962) stated that an objective must identify the expected behavior in detail, the conditions in which the behavior is to be displayed, and the criteria for judging students' performance. Marzano and Kendall (1996, p. 8) contend that an example of a behavioral objective following Mager's definition would be: "At the end of a 50-minute period of instruction, students will be able to complete eight out of ten problems in two-column addition within a five-minute period." Not surprisingly, teachers felt overwhelmed by the sheer number of objectives required to specify educational outcomes, and the movement failed. The focus seemed to be more on accounting than on teaching, and the voluminous paperwork took too much time away from instruction.

What Is the Standards Movement?

Educators and the public in general have been calling for school reform since the publication of *A Nation at Risk* in 1983 by the National Commission on Excellence in Education. The modern standards movement really began with the release of this damaging report on public education. In light of its findings and recommendations, there was a growing sentiment that the development of standards held the promise for improving education. Once the report appeared, members of the business community shared their concerns about students not being academically prepared to enter the workforce, and politicians and many educators began to support the standards movement.

The standards movement gained further impetus with the publication of the book *National Standards in American Education: A Citizen's Guide*, by former Assistant Secretary of Education Diane Ravitch, in 1995. Ravitch (as cited in Marzano & Kendall, 1996) asserted that standards would improve academic achievement by clearly defining what knowledge and skills would be taught and what students would have to do to demonstrate that they had mastered them.

Various national professional organizations established standards that they hoped all states would adopt. But despite these efforts, most states eventually created their own standards, as well as the high-stakes tests that would assess students' ability to meet them. Since each state developed its own standards, the terminology, expectations, degree of rigor, and methods of assessment varied tremendously. In other words, the widening standards movement lacked standardization.

Today, even though educators are accustomed to the idea of standards and have heard the mantra "Begin with the end in mind," they are somewhat confused. They don't necessarily know how their own states define standards. Many states use the term *content standard* to describe a statement that answers the question "What should students know or be able to do?" Other states use the term *performance standard* to describe a statement that answers the question "How good is good enough?" (Solomon, 2002). Some states use the term *performance indicators* to describe the skill-defining parts of content standards. Other states use terms such as *descriptors, proficiencies, outcomes, elements, competencies, benchmarks, expectations,* or *criteria*. Some states target multiple grade levels with clustered standards, such as K–2 standards or 4–5 standards. Other states use one standard, such as "Students will develop a persuasive piece of writing," across all grade levels and use benchmarks at each grade level to describe the specific performances students should be able to achieve. Some states provide specific details for each standard and benchmarks similar to the behavioral objectives of the 1960s, while other states provide a general goal that allows teachers to determine the specifics.

All standards are treated as if they are equally important, even though some are much more important than others. Teachers, therefore, are not sure which standards to emphasize when preparing their students to take the state's high-stakes tests. Even though state tests are used to measure whether or not students meet the standards, Fuhrman, Resnick, and Shepard (2009, p. 28) have found that "the tests now used by states to measure student proficiency are often a grab bag of items only loosely matched to state standards." It is apparent that despite the use of standards throughout the country, the implementation and results are not standardized.

What Are National and International Standards?

By 2009, two factors had converged to put into motion a serious effort to develop national, "internationally benchmarked" standards. The first was mounting concern about the poor performance of U.S. high school students on international assessments in math and science (National Center for Education Statistics, 2009). The second was concern about the inconsistent proficiency standards that states had established to satisfy the requirements of the No Child Left Behind law, which was introduced in 2001. Finn and Petrilli (2009, p. 31) noted that there was "so much state-to-state variation as to turn the promise of results-based accountability into an illusion" (p. 31). Gerald Tirozzi, the executive director of the National Association of Secondary Principals, observed, "We as a nation have no aversion to national standards. We set them for everything—food, cars, toys, pet food, gas consumption, and on and on. Why not," he proposed, set "national standards for all students—at a minimum—in reading and math?" (2009, p. 23).

The National Governors Association and the Council of Chief State School Officers, in partnership with Achieve, ACT, and the College Board, took the lead in initiating a national standards process. By September of 2009, forty-eight states and the District of Columbia had joined the Common Core State Standards Initiative, whose purpose was to develop national standards that would be internationally benchmarked. These standards were to be "research- and evidence-based, internationally benchmarked, aligned with college and work expectations, and [would] include rigorous content and skills" (Common Core State Standards Initiative, 2009). But the creation of national standards to influence how teachers teach and how students learn would be just the first step. According to Fuhrman et al. (2009, p. 28), "curricula, tests, textbooks, lesson plans, and teachers' on-the-job training will all have to be revised to reinforce the standards. Only then will these new 'common-core standards' serve as the organizing principle for U.S. public education."

Also in 2009, the U.S. Department of Education announced a $4-billion federal stimulus grant program called Race to the Top, which encouraged innovation and focused on methods to help struggling schools. States applying for the grants were to be judged on nineteen education reform criteria. "Standards and Assessments" was the first broad category in which states would have to demonstrate improvement. The following draft criteria were listed under this category:

- Developing and adopting common standards
- Developing and implementing common, high-quality assessments
- Making the transition to enhanced standards and high-quality assessments (U.S. Department of Education, 2009)

The intent was to make national standards and assessments more rigorous and more universal so that no student and no state would be left behind in the race to the top.

Are There Too Many Standards?

One of the greatest challenges for teachers is the sheer number of standards they are expected to address. Most states have mandated more content than can be covered in the K–12 system. Marzano (2006) notes that researchers at Mid-continent Research for Education and Learning (McREL) examined national- and state-level standards documents across fourteen subject areas and identified some two hundred standards and 3,093 benchmarks. The researchers asked teachers how long it would take to address the content specified in the standards. They then compared the teachers' responses with the amount of time that is available for classroom instruction. They concluded that teachers would need 71 percent more instructional time to address the mandated content in the standards documents. Marzano says, "Another way of looking at this is that schooling, as currently configured, would have to be extended from kindergarten to grade 21 or 22 to accommodate all the standards and benchmarks in the national documents" (2006, p. 13). Teachers feel overwhelmed trying to address all the standards, engage in meaningful and thoughtful instruction, and implement a variety of interventions to help struggling students.

Directly related to the overabundance of standards is the extent of the content presented in textbooks. Schmidt, McKnight, and Raizen (1996, as cited in Marzano, 2006) reported that German and Japanese students outperformed U.S. students significantly on the Third International Mathematics and Science Study, even though their textbooks covered significantly fewer topics than mathematics and science books in the United States. They found that "U.S. mathematics textbooks attempt to cover 175 percent as many topics as do German textbooks and 350 percent as many topics as do Japanese textbooks. Similarly, U.S. science textbooks attempt to cover more than nine times as many topics as do German textbooks and more than four times as many topics as do Japanese textbooks" (1996, as cited in Marzano, 2006, p. 13).

Textbook companies in the United States depend on the adoption cycles in each state. Because it would be financially impossible to create a textbook in each content area that targets each state's standards, many companies include multiple concepts from as many states as possible and then provide a supplement or key for each state's standards. Unfortunately, this makes textbooks very large and expensive, and many teachers think that they must "teach the whole textbook" regardless of whether a lesson addresses their specific state standards. Teachers sometimes spend unnecessary time covering material for other states and then do not have sufficient time to address the material related to their own state standards.

Could educators today learn a lesson from the failed behavioral objectives movement of the 1960s? If the national standards movement succeeds in creating standards that address only the most critical knowledge and skills that students will need, the textbook industry might follow.

Before the standards movement, many teachers focused on units they enjoyed and devoted little time to units they did not like. Sometimes, they would even skip entire units or chapters because they ran out of time. But today, teachers feel obligated to teach everything in their curriculum and in their textbook, because "it could be on the test." This pressure permeates many classrooms. Often, schools require teachers to teach prescriptive lessons to all students on a specific day. Teachers are expected to follow a rigid pacing guide to prepare students to take benchmark tests to determine if they are on track to pass the high-stakes standardized tests. The same schools and districts that require teachers to adhere to prescriptive curriculum guidelines with specific pacing time frames may also have a school goal of differentiating instruction. It is challenging to take extra time to meet the diverse needs of struggling students if teachers feel pressured to meet deadlines. Benchmark or interim tests yield feedback to guide future instruction, but time has to be available to provide remediation to students who have not mastered the material. Otherwise, the results of the next short-cycle assessment will show, once again, that they are not ready for the final test.

Drake and Burns (2004) believe many teachers feel like they are teaching in a pressure cooker. The demands on teachers to cover the standards and on students to perform well on standardized measures can be overwhelming. Educators sometimes avoid using engaging curriculum units or interactive instructional strategies because they feel they cannot spend the time on them. They are afraid they will get off their pacing schedule and their students will score poorly on the periodic benchmark assessments. Unfortunately, struggling students are required to take *more* practice tests, so there is rarely time for anything other than test preparation.

One way to adhere to the standards and to make them come alive is to integrate the curriculum by "chunking" the standards together into meaningful clusters within and across disciplines. Interdisciplinary teaching accomplishes this goal and motivates students. For example, a unit on Egypt could focus on learning language arts, art, math, science, and social studies in the context of studying the country. Chapter 4 describes how to create performance tasks to make the curriculum more relevant to students.

What Are Power Standards?

One method that would reduce the number of standards would be to identify the "power standards." The term *power standard* is associated with Douglas Reeves (2003). Reeves notes that states first introduced standards in the early 1990s and then continued to add more content over the years. In response to the increasing demands, "some districts have created pacing charts and curriculum maps, hoping that the right combination of time management and exceedingly rapid speech will provide the necessary coverage of standards and curriculum" (Reeves, 2003, p. 110). But Reeves suggests that "a more thoughtful approach" is to focus on power standards—those that possess the qualities of endurance, leverage, and necessity for the next level of instruction. He explains the first two qualities as follows:

> The property of endurance implies that the standard has lasting value. Some standards, such as those relating to reading comprehension, writing skill, and understanding of mathematical relationships, provide students knowledge and skills that will endure throughout their academic careers and beyond. Other standards, by contrast, have limited endurance and provide limited utility after a single grade in school.

> The principle of leverage is related to the application of a standard to multiple academic disciplines. For example, student proficiency in nonfiction writing is directly related to student success in reading, mathematics, social studies, and science. Student success in the creation and interpretation of tables, charts, and graphs is related to student success in mathematics, social studies, and science. Thus, these skills with the property of leverage deserve far greater emphasis than many other standards with limited relevance to other subjects. (2003, p. 110)

As for the third quality, necessity for the next level of instruction, certain standards are building blocks for the next course or school year. If students cannot master the standards in one grade level, they will not be able to understand the standards that lie ahead.

Ainsworth (2007) adds that power standards must reflect state assessments. He explains:

> Power standards reflect the collective wisdom of educators who first use their professional judgment and experience to select those specific standards they consider critical for students to fully understand and be able to demonstrate. They then cross-reference those initial selections with their state assessment data and state assessment guidelines to make sure their choices match those standards emphasized the most on the state assessment. (p. 86)

Power standards are vertically aligned from kindergarten to grade 12 so that there is a "flow" of key standards throughout the grades. When all the teachers know the power standards, the district establishes consistency, because everyone focuses on the essential learning outcomes. Teachers still need to teach other standards, but they work together as a group to prioritize the learning outcomes by determining their curricular focus (Ainsworth, 2007).

Unpacking and Repacking the Standards

Standards-based instruction and assessment embed the language and the concepts of the standards into the entire teaching process. Teachers start with the target—the standards—and then plan backward. They develop the assessments that will measure whether the students have met or exceeded the standards. Then they plan their curriculum and develop different instructional strategies that will help their students attain mastery.

In planning backward from the standards, the first step is to analyze precisely what concepts and skills they encompass. For example, a fourth-grade language arts writing standard from the Georgia Department of Education (2010) states: "The student demonstrates competence in a variety of genres." Included under the standard is the specific substandard "The student produces a persuasive essay." This sounds very simple, but the multiple performance indicators listed under that substandard can be quite complex:

The student produces a persuasive essay that:

   a   Engages the reader by establishing a context, creating a speaker's voice, and otherwise developing reader interest.

   b   States a clear position.

   c   Supports a position with relevant evidence.

   d   Excludes extraneous details and inappropriate information.

   e   Creates an organizing structure appropriate to a specific purpose, audience, and context.

   f   Provides a sense of closure to the writing. (Georgia Department of Education, 2010, ELA4W2)

The fifth-grade writing standard includes the same performance indicators for the persuasive essay as the fourth-grade standard (although in a slightly different order) and adds two more:

   g   Addresses reader concerns.

   h   Raises the level of language using appropriate strategies (word choice). (Georgia Department of Education, 2010, ELA5W2)

The verbiage alone is overwhelming for fourth- and fifth-grade students, as well as many teachers. To be able to teach the standards and assess students' progress toward meeting them, it is first necessary to "unpack" or "unwrap" them. To do so, teams of educators analyze the nouns and verbs to make a list of what students need to *know* (key concepts and important understandings) and a list of what students need to *do* (key skills or procedural knowledge). These lists help teachers see specifically what they will need to *teach*. The next step for most school districts is to look at the big ideas or conceptual understandings targeted by the standards and pose several essential questions to ask students at the beginning of the unit to guide their learning.

Once this is accomplished, another crucial process needs to be carried out so that all these concepts, nouns, and verbs make sense. Too many frustrated teachers undergo the unpacking process but still ask the question, "How do I teach this?" The answer is to "repack" the standards—that is, organize the various indicators into teachable "chunks" and arrange them in an instructional sequence that is developmentally appropriate for the students. As introduced by Burke (2006), the practice of repacking the standards helps teachers to create an instructional plan for targeting each performance indicator included in the standard. The plan provides progressions of learning to help students know not only *what* to do but also *how* to do it and *when* to do it.

The repacking process is both visual and kinesthetic. It involves teams of teachers using large chart paper and three different sizes and colors of sticky notes. Teachers also need a copy of one target or power standard and all the performance indicators included under the standard. Since each state has created its own standards, the terminology may vary. States may use terms such as *elements*, *descriptors*, *criteria*, *benchmarks*, *grade-level expectations*, or *competencies* instead of *performance indicators*. It is important for teachers to use the terminology preferred by their own state departments of education to avoid confusion. Figure 1.1 shows the steps for repacking the standards.

Step 1: Target a Standard

Select a target or power standard and review all the performance indicators included under the standard.

Step 2: Chunk the Main Categories

Chunk the main categories of the performance indicators by identifying key verbs, nouns, and phrases.

Write the main categories on large (4" × 6") sticky notes and then place them on poster paper.

Step 3: Sequence the Order for Teaching

Review the main categories on the 4" × 6" sticky notes and place them in the logical sequence necessary to teach the information to the students.

Step 4: Include All Other Performance Indicators

Write all the remaining performance indicators on square (3" × 3") sticky notes and place them under the appropriate main categories.

Step 5: Add Clarifying Information

Add definitions, examples, symbols, formulas, pictures, or "kid" language on small (2" × 2" or 2" × 1.5") sticky notes to explain the performance indicators more clearly.

Step 6: Review Teaching Strategies

Work with a team to review and share appropriate instructional strategies that will help teachers implement the standard successfully.

Figure 1.1: Repacking the standards.

In step 1, the team members select the target standard and then review all the performance indicators listed under it. In step 2, they write the key verbs, nouns, and phrases of the performance indicators on 4″ × 6″ sticky notes. For example, the fourth-grade persuasive essay standard described earlier states that students will produce a persuasive essay that "engages the reader by establishing a context, creating a speaker's voice, and otherwise developing reader interest." Teachers could chunk the main idea of all those performance indicators and write "Engage the Reader" on one 4″ × 6″ sticky note. The other indicators that follow—"establishing a context, creating a speaker's voice, and developing reader interest"—are specific *methods* one could use to engage the reader. They will be reserved for step 4.

Most standards and their correlating performance indicators are not written in the sequential order that teachers would use to introduce a process such as writing a persuasive essay. It is often necessary to rearrange the chunks to make the process developmentally appropriate for the age group and the ability level of the students. In step 3, the team decides on the sequence in which to teach the main categories. Teachers who are working together to repack their standards may disagree about what would be the best sequence, but the conversations will help the entire group analyze the flow of the process more carefully. For example, some teachers might want to begin teaching the persuasive essay by asking students to engage their readers by motivating them to want to read the essay. Since "engage the reader" is listed first in the fourth-grade standard, this could seem like a logical place to begin. Other teachers, however, might believe that the fifth indicator in the standard—creating an organizing structure—should be introduced first, so that the students can write an appropriate lead to fit the purpose or context of their essays. Once the team has settled on a starting point, the teachers will rearrange the rest of the indicators accordingly. Even though the team may achieve consensus about the best order in which to teach the essay-writing process, individual teachers will vary the order and adjust the categories to accommodate their own teaching styles as well as the learning needs of their students.

In step 4, teachers turn to the performance indicators that were not selected as the main categories in step 2. They write all of these remaining performance indicators on square sticky notes of a second color and size (3″ × 3″) and place them under the appropriate main categories. For example, under the large sticky note with the main category "Engage the Reader," the teachers would place three 3″ × 3″ sticky notes on which they have written the methods for engaging the reader: "Establish a Context," "Create a Speaker's Voice," and "Develop Reader Interest." In this step, it is important to include all the words and phrases addressed in the standard and performance indicators, since these are the terms considered important for all students to know.

The Language of the Standards

Even though all states probably have a standard or goal of "writing a persuasive essay," the vocabulary used in the standard could vary from state to state. Many teachers develop a vocabulary list of key terms from the standard and descriptors and review and discuss them before teaching the standard. When teachers preteach or "frontload" the vocabulary, students are better able to understand the concepts when they are introduced. As they teach a process such as writing a persuasive essay, they include synonyms next to the language of their state standard to show students various terms that are similar. An example would be: "Use a hook (*motivator, lead, grabber*) to engage your readers." Or "Underline the base (*root*) word."

Since high-stakes state tests should be correlated to the state standards, they will use these standards-based vocabulary words. Each state may have as many as ten different textbooks from different publishers adopted by districts, but it will be the language of the standards (LOTS)—*not* the language of the textbooks (LOTT)—that will be embedded throughout the mandated tests that determine promotion or retention.

Table 1.1 shows a list of vocabulary words derived from both the fourth- and fifth-grade standards and performance indicators for the persuasive essay that were quoted on page 10.

Table 1.1: Language of the Standard for a Persuasive Essay

Nouns	Verbs	Phrases
Context	Engage	Speaker's voice
Voice	Establish	Reader interest
Interest	Create	Clear position
Position	Develop	Relevant evidence
Evidence	State	Organizing structure
Details	Support	Specific purpose
Information	Address	Reader concerns
Structure	Exclude	Extraneous details
Purpose	Provide	Inappropriate information
Audience	Raise	Sense of closure
Concerns		Level of language
Closure		Appropriate strategies
Language		Word choice
Strategies		

Step 5 is probably the most important step in the process of repacking the standards. This is the step that asks teachers to go beyond the language of the standards and use small (2″ × 2″ or 2″ × 1.5″) sticky notes in a third color to add clarifying definitions, examples, symbols, or formulas to make the standard more "kid-friendly." Most fourth- or fifth-graders will have problems with the robust vocabulary of the persuasive essay standard and descriptors. Even if teachers frontload the vocabulary words for weeks in advance, students will struggle doing their persuasive essay when they see the words *context, extraneous,* or *closure* late at night while trying to finish their homework. Students need to see an easier, more age-appropriate word or phrase, or perhaps a picture, that conveys the LOTS more clearly. For example, next to "Exclude extraneous details," a phrase that is not used by most fourth-graders in their daily conversations, the small sticky note could say, "Leave out things that are not needed," "Throw out the extra stuff," "Cross out irrelevant things," or "Eliminate things that don't support the topic." The more synonyms used, the better the chance of helping students struggling with language problems to understand the concepts.

Another reason to add clarifying information is that sometimes the performance indicators are too abstract for students to understand. For example, asking students to "create an organizing structure appropriate to a specific purpose, audience, and context" might not make sense to them if they are not familiar with types of organizing structures. Teachers can use the small sticky notes to add examples of organizing structures such as "posing and answering a question," "chronological order," "similarities and differences," and "cause and effect" to help students translate broad categories into concrete steps. Another example of a somewhat vague performance indicator is the one that asks students to "raise their level of language using appropriate strategies." Many students might think that this means they should use big words. The small sticky notes could specify "descriptive words," "sensory details," and "figurative language" and give examples of each so that students truly understand what it means to "raise their level of language." These additional words and phrases should be added to the vocabulary list because they support the students' understanding of the important concepts.

The details that teachers provide in step 5 provide the kid-friendly scaffolding that many students need in order to accomplish the task successfully. For younger students, pictures are always appropriate, and all students welcome synonyms or examples. Here are some examples of scaffolding from different subjects:

- Label the triangle. △
- Draw a square. □
- Write a salutation (greeting) for your letter.
- Give the mean (average) of your two scores.
- Analyze data using measures of central tendency (mean, median, mode).

Reviewing Strategies

In step 6 of the process, teachers share ideas for instruction. During their team meetings or common planning periods, teachers demonstrate instructional strategies that have worked for them. All teachers learn how to expand their repertoire of differentiated strategies to meet the diverse needs of all their students. The process of introducing the persuasive essay to fourth- or fifth-grade students could take weeks or months. During this time, teachers will continue to meet with their teams to design assessments (as will be discussed in the next section and in later chapters), review the results, and discuss how to modify their instruction.

How Should School Teams Develop Standards-Based Assessments?

Once the standard and all its performance indicators (elements, benchmarks, competencies, expectations, criteria) have been chunked, arranged sequentially, and made more kid-friendly, it is time for the teacher team to create a graphic organizer: a checklist. Burke (2006) describes the *teacher checklist* as a linear roadmap that helps teachers plan their building blocks of instruction and assign a time frame that will enable them to appropriately address all the parts of a process such as writing a persuasive essay.

Teachers will later adapt their checklist into a *student checklist* to guide their students in organizing a big task, like writing a five-paragraph persuasive essay, into more manageable steps or mini-tasks. It is important that teachers organize the standard themselves before they attempt to teach it to their students. Many students, particularly in the elementary grades, will not recognize the nouns and verbs embedded in the standard and will not have the skills or procedural knowledge necessary to write a five-paragraph persuasive essay without various degrees of support.

Student checklists have another function: they are used to *assess* student progress toward meeting standards. Using the language of the standards, the teacher teams devise questions to ask students in order to determine which steps they have completed. The students go through each question, fill in their answers, and mark the column indicating whether or not they have completed the step. The checklists provide immediate feedback to the teacher and show what areas need clarification or additional instruction. Moreover, checklists enable students to work independently and monitor their own progress because they know the expectations for quality work.

Chapter 5 is entirely devoted to checklists and will go into greater detail about how to construct and use them. But because checklists play such an important role in instruction and assessment, they are being introduced here, and examples of them will appear in this and the following chapters. Figure 1.2 is a checklist that the fourth- and fifth-grade team created for the persuasive essay standard. From this example, we can see how a checklist serves the dual role of instructional roadmap and performance assessment.

Persuasive Essay Checklist

Standard: The student demonstrates competence in writing a persuasive essay.

Task: Students will write a persuasive essay using either "posing and answering a question" or "cause and effect" as their organizing structure.

Performance Indicators	Not Yet	Yes
Did you select an organizing structure? (Check the row for the one you used.)		
Did you pose a question? For example: Should people be allowed to smoke in public? What is your question? _____		
Did you have a cause and an effect? What is your cause? _____ For example: My grandfather smoked cigarettes. What was the effect? _____ For example: He died from lung cancer.		

Figure 1.2: Persuasive essay checklist.

continued on next page →

	Not Yet	Yes

Did you engage your reader?

Did you establish a context for your persuasive essay?

What is it? _____

Does your essay provide a point of view?

What is it? _____

Did you grab your readers' attention? (hook, grabber, motivator, or lead)

What was it? _____

Did you state a clear position?

What is your position?

For example: I am against smoking in public places.

_____

_____

_____

Did you state your main idea, topic sentence, or focus?

What is it? _____

Did you support your position?

Did you present relevant evidence (facts or statistics)?

What facts or statistics did you use?

For example: Thousands die from smoking related illnesses every year.

List some of your facts: _____

_____

Did you use any appeals? (emotional appeals/personal experiences)

How will this help you support your position? _____

_____

Did you address the reader's concerns?

Did you debate on paper the opposing arguments?

What is a possible opposing argument that could refute (be against) your position? _____

_____

	Not Yet	Yes
Did you raise your level of language using appropriate strategies?		
Did you use concrete or descriptive words (vocabulary; adjectives and adverbs)? Examples: _____ Did you use figurative language and/or sensory detail (similes and metaphors)? Examples: _____		
Did you provide closure?		
Did you restate/rephrase the thesis, summarize main points, and state personal beliefs/feelings? How did you reference your hook/lead/motivator? _____ _____		
Did you exclude extraneous details and inappropriate information?		
Did you edit and delete unrelated and extra information?		

Created by Marva Bell, Lori Higgs, LaKeia King, and Shanon Melson; Carrollton Middle School; Carrollton City Schools; Carrollton, Georgia. Used with permission.

Students will not always have the scaffolding that the checklist provides, but hopefully, they will remember the process. The fourth-grade student who struggles with writing an essay will continue to write persuasive essays throughout high school and college. If a school system uses K–12 vertical teams to develop common assessments in the form of checklists built around the power standards, students will build on their early foundation and meet and exceed standards throughout their school experiences.

Final Thoughts

Standards-based teaching involves embedding the language and concepts of the standards into teachers' curriculum development, instructional strategies, and assessments. Standards-based assessments truly reflect the phrase "begin with the end in mind," because the standards are the target. Valid and reliable standards-based common assessments are the roadmap that teachers need to use to "plan backward" and target their instruction toward the ultimate outcome. The early hope that standards would improve students' academic achievement will finally be realized when rigorous standards-based assessments created by teacher teams truly drive all instruction toward common goals.

Concluding Exercises

Reflections on Standards

1 Are standards improving education? Why or why not?

2 Rate your state's standards and standardized tests compared to those of other states. Explain your rating.

3 Do you think national and international standards should replace state standards? Explain.

4 Why are standards-based assessments more important than just standards?

Action Steps

List three action steps you plan to take related to teaching and assessing your standards.

Step 1:

Step 2:

Step 3:

2

The Balanced Assessment Model: When Formative Meets Summative

Assessment is a broad term that can be looked at from many dimensions, including instructional purpose. The instructional purpose of a formative assessment is to provide feedback *during* the learning process; the instructional purpose of a summative assessment is to make a final judgment at the *end* of the learning process.

What Is the Difference Between Assessment and Evaluation?

Assessment is the process of gathering evidence of student learning to inform instructional decisions. If the evidence is accurate and timely, educators can use it to support student learning. Assessment consists of all the tools that teachers use to collect information about student learning and instructional effectiveness. Teachers use tests, presentations, observations, and class work to assess student learning. *Evaluation* is the procedure for collecting information and making a judgment about it. For example, standardized test scores, dropout and graduation rates, and promotion and retention rates are used to evaluate the success of a high school (Carey, 2001, as cited in Ataya, 2007). Assessment is an ongoing process that occurs daily, whereas evaluation often occurs at the end of an assessment cycle.

When people think of types of assessment, they usually think about formative and summative, but these categories relate only to the purpose of the assessment. According to Ataya (2007), assessment can be categorized on the basis of seven dimensions, as shown in table 2.1 (page 20).

Table 2.1: Assessment Dimensions and Categories

Dimension	Category
Method of Development	Teacher made
	Standardized
Nature of the Task	Traditional
	Alternative
Instructional Purpose	Formative
	Summative
Level of Formality	Formal
	Informal
Grading Standard	Criterion referenced
	Norm referenced
Type of Item	Selected response
	Constructed response
Type of Scoring	Objective
	Subjective

Source: Based on Ataya, R. L. (2007). Policy and technical considerations for classroom assessment. In P. Jones, J. F. Carr, and R. L. Ataya (Eds.), *A pig don't get fatter the more you weigh it: Classroom assessments that work* (p. 76). New York: Teachers College Press.

What Is Assessment Literacy?

Many educators took one preservice course in educational measurement in college. They learned how to calculate the mean, the median, and the mode for their grade books and thought that *assessment, evaluation, testing, grading,* and *measurement* all meant basically the same thing. Who could have predicted that education reform in the twenty-first century would focus on analyzing assessment data to improve student achievement? Today's teachers need to become assessment literate to understand the comprehensive picture of assessment preparation and practice. Stiggins, Arter, Chappuis, and Chappuis (2004) believe that teachers should be able to design accurate assessment tools and use the assessment responses to make informed decisions. Teachers must acquire the knowledge and skills necessary for monitoring students' progress toward mastery of learning standards. Erkens (2009, p. 14) explains that teachers should ask the right questions, analyze the answers "to find the learners *where they are,* and then work *to take them where they need to be.* We do this through dynamic, interactive instruction, appropriate feedback, and strategies that involve the learners as key decision makers in the process." The ultimate goal is for all students to achieve mastery of the learning expectations.

What Is Formative Assessment?

For many years, educators did not distinguish between formative and summative assessment because they could not see the practical implications of the distinction for classroom teaching. Since the 1960s, however, educators have begun discussing how the distinctions between the formative and summative roles of assessment could influence instructional decisions. Michael Scriven wrote a groundbreaking essay in 1967 in which he contrasted summative evaluation with formative evaluation. Popham (2008) says, "We continue to see formative assessment as a way to improve the caliber of still-underway instructional activities and summative assessment as a way to determine the effectiveness of already-completed instructional activities" (p. 4).

The tendency in education today is to regard formative assessment as assessment *for* learning, because it informs teachers and students, and summative assessment as assessment *of* learning, because it informs the stakeholders (parents, administrators, and public officials) about how well teachers and students have performed. These two terms categorize assessment according to its instructional purpose. Popham (2008) observes that formative assessment involves a series of "carefully considered, distinguishable acts on the part of teachers *or* students *or* both. Some of these acts involve educational assessments, but the assessments play a role in the process—they are not the process itself" (p. 7). He says that instead of using the term *formative test,* educators should recognize that the test is only one part of the multistep formative assessment process that is necessary to improve student learning.

The underlying idea of formative assessment is to use minute-to-minute and day-by-day evidence to adjust instruction (Wiliam, 2007). Black and Wiliam (1998) reviewed the research and concluded that regular use of classroom formative assessment would raise student achievement by 0.4 to 0.7 standard deviations. That would be enough to place the United States in the top five countries in the international rankings for math achievement (Wiliam, 2007). Formative assessment uses informal techniques like conversations with students, class interactions, questioning, daily work, observation, interviews, conferences, and graphic organizers, as well as more formal techniques like quizzes, performance assessments, and portfolio assessments to monitor student progress and modify instruction accordingly (Ataya, 2007). Many formative assessments are not graded but are used instead as methods of feedback to help students improve their work before the final summative evaluation. When football coaches are conducting practices to prepare for the big game on Friday night, their assessment of the players' performance is formative. The score on the scoreboard at the end of the game and all the statistics are final or summative.

Why Is Feedback an Important Component of Assessment?

Feedback is the heart and soul of formative assessment. In the *Handbook on Formative and Summative Evaluation of Student Learning* (Bloom, Hastings, & Madaus, 1971, as cited in Guskey, 2007/2008), Benjamin Bloom and his colleagues "described the benefits of offering students regular feedback on their learning progress through formative classroom assessments" (Guskey, 2007/2008, p. 28). Guskey notes that formative assessments "pinpoint for both students and teachers what concepts and skills have been learned well and what learning problems still exist" (pp. 28–29). If the instructional purpose of the assessment is formative, teachers will engage in an ongoing process that involves giving specific feedback and directions to students as they proceed toward the instructional goal. The feedback is intended to help students reflect on their own learning and adjust their strategies as needed in order to meet or exceed the standards and achieve deeper understanding of the important concepts.

Hattie and Timperley (2007, as cited in O'Connor, 2009) found that the greatest benefits from feedback occurred when students received feedback related to how to do a task more effectively. Their meta-analysis included 196 studies and 6,972 effect sizes and showed that feedback in classrooms had an average effect size of 0.79—twice the average effect. Marzano (2009, p. 119) explains that "an average effect size reports the results of all of the included studies to tell us whether or not [the practice being examined] improves student achievement and, if so, by how much." Hattie and Timperley point out that teachers must use feedback skillfully to develop a classroom climate that encourages complex judgments and deep understanding of content and concepts. They also discuss the challenge of "having exquisite timing to provide feedback before frustration takes over" (Hattie & Timperley, 2007, as cited in O'Connor, 2009, p. 123). Effective teachers strike a balance between trying to rescue a student by giving too much feedback too soon and letting the student "sink or swim" on his or her own.

Some educators recommend never providing both comments (feedback) and a grade on students' work. They believe that most of the time, students will ignore the feedback and focus only on the grade. Vatterott (2009) notes that good oral and written feedback on homework requires back-and-forth dialogue between the teacher and the student. For many teachers, however, providing feedback without grades is a new way of communicating progress. Vatterott observes, "They've never done school without grades, and for many of them, grades are the only way they know to give feedback. Letters and numbers are easy and fast, and they make up a language everyone *thinks* they understand" (2009, p. 113).

O'Connor (2009) believes it is important for educators to understand the difference between feedback and guidance. He explains that "*feedback* provides descriptive information about what the student did, while *guidance* provides information about what the student should do to improve. Students need both, but the sequence in which they are provided is very important" (p. 125). O'Connor says that educators and parents tend to provide guidance before feedback. "The problem," he points out, "with giving guidance first is that the learner may have a defensive reaction and not really hear the feedback, but if we give descriptive feedback first, the learner is much more likely to be open to—and act upon—the guidance" (2009, p. 125). Once students learn to process the feedback and reflect metacognitively on their work, they should be able to move beyond teacher-generated guidance and learn how to guide themselves to make necessary improvements on their own.

What Are Corrective Interventions?

According to Bloom and his colleagues (Bloom, Hastings, & Madaus, 1971, as cited in Guskey, 2007/2008), formative progress checks must help teachers to identify each student's individual learning difficulties and to offer specific remediation strategies to correct the problems. Some students take the initiative and correct their own problems by trying different strategies. Most students, however, depend on the teacher to help them correct their misunderstandings. Bloom and his colleagues emphasized that the corrective strategies

> will be effective *only if* they are qualitatively different from the original instruction. Having students repeat a process that has already proven unsuccessful is unlikely to yield any better results the second time around. Effective corrective activities provide students with alternative pathways to learning success, adapted to meet their individual learning needs and interests. (Guskey, 2007/2008, p. 29)

The goal of differentiated instruction and response to intervention (RTI) is to offer a repertoire of teaching and assessment strategies to meet the needs of all students. Guskey (2007/2008, p. 30) notes that "the best corrective activities involve a change in format, organization, or method of presentation" and should "engage students differently in learning." Table 2.2 lists various instructional interventions teachers can use to remediate students who experience difficulties during the formative assessment progress checks. The formative assessments highlight a student's difficulties, but the next step is to find multiple strategies to solve the problems.

Table 2.2: Corrective Interventions

Reteaching	Cooperative Groups	Individual Work
Charts Graphs Graphic organizers Videos/DVDs/films Role playing Mock trial Demonstration Exemplars	Expert jigsaw (each member becomes an expert in one area and teaches others) Simulation games Learning centers Peer tutoring Projects Performances	Individual tutoring Study guides Workbooks Alternative textbooks (trade books, big books) Computer programs Learning kits (manipulatives)

Source: Based on Guskey, T. R. (2007/2008). The rest of the story. *Educational Leadership* (65)4, 30–32.

What Is Summative Assessment?

Summative assessment occurs when teachers evaluate a final product. It usually takes place at the end of a chapter, a unit of study, a benchmark period, a quarter, a course, a semester, or an academic year. Summative assessments report the students' final results to the students themselves, their parents, and the administration, as well as the school district, the state, and the national government. These final results become the data that are used for many purposes, including the promotion and retention of students and the evaluation of individual schools and districts. Summative assessments serve as assessments *of* learning, because their purpose is to support the assignment of final grades or levels of proficiency related to course outcomes or state standards.

Ainsworth and Viegut (2006) describe summative assessments as often stand-alone final assessments used to measure students' understanding of units in a textbook or to determine whether students have met the standards or learning objectives during a grading period or course of study. They point out that "since these assessments take place after all instruction and student learning have ended, they are summative in both design and intent" (Ainsworth & Viegut, 2006, p. 24). Because summative assessments come at the end of a learning period, they don't usually include descriptive feedback telling students what they need to do to improve. The only feedback comes in the form of a letter grade, percentage grade, pass/fail grade, or label such as "exceeds standards" or "needs improvement." If teachers offer comments, students will probably focus only on the final grade and not appreciate the feedback because it is too late to change the results.

Ainsworth and Viegut (2006) note that since all the learning activities related to the targeted standards have concluded, "the results of summative assessments are not used to improve student understanding for *current* students. Instead, teachers typically use these assessment results to judge the effectiveness of their teaching practices and to improve instruction of those standards for *future* students" (p. 24). In addition, schools and districts use the results to determine which programs worked and which didn't and thus should be either improved or eliminated in the coming year. Summative assessments also provide the public and policymakers with a sense of the results of their investment in education and give educators a forum for proving instruction works—or does not work.

Why Does the Balanced Assessment Model Work?

According to Stiggins et al. (2004, p. 25), "a balanced assessment system takes advantage of assessment *of* learning and assessment *for* learning; each can make essential contributions. When both are present in the system, assessment becomes more than just an index of school success. It also serves as the cause of that success." The integration of both assessment for learning (formative) and assessment of learning (summative) is essential. If the teacher embeds the language of the standards (LOTS) in all his or her formative and summative assessments, students know the expectations for quality work on both teacher-made assessments and high-stakes standardized tests.

Many educators associate formative assessments with anything done in the classroom and summative assessments with standardized tests. But the summative assessment process is a critical component of classroom assessment because it is used at the end of a learning experience to make a final evaluation and assign a grade. Students may write three rough drafts of a research paper and use multiple checklists and practice rubrics, but eventually they have to turn in a final paper for a grade. If students are asked to write a rough draft so that the teacher can read it, give feedback, and adjust teaching and learning in real time, it is part of the formative assessment process. If the students are asked to write the final paper so that the teacher can make a value judgment as to whether it meets the expectations of quality work, then it is a part of the summative assessment process. The *purpose* of the assessment, the *timing* of the assessment, the course requirements, and the state standards determine whether the assessment is classified as formative or summative. Some words and phrases that are associated with formative assessment are *process driven*, *practice*, *feedback*, *work in progress*, *do-overs*, *beginning of course*, and *not graded*. Some words and phrases that are associated with summative assessment are *product driven*, *last efforts*, *results based*, *outcome based*, *last judgment*, *end of course*, and *final grade*.

In the balanced assessment model presented in table 2.3, the same assessment could be classified as formative during the initial teaching and learning process and as summative during the final stages of the grading period. The language of the standards (nouns, verbs, concepts, big ideas) should be embedded in both types of assessment to ensure that they are correlated to the state standards.

Formative and summative assessments support each other and should be viewed as in sync. They can even be the *exact same thing*—only the purpose and the timing of the assessment determine its label. Formative assessments provide the training wheels that allow students to practice and gain confidence while riding their bikes around the enclosed school parking lot. Once the training wheels come off, the students face their summative assessment as they ride off into the sunset on only two wheels, prepared to navigate the twists and turns of the road to arrive safely at their final destination.

Table 2.3: The Balanced Assessment Model

Formative Assessment Process	Summative Assessment Process
Assessment *for* Learning	Assessment *of* Learning
Purpose: Provide ongoing feedback to *improve* learning	Purpose: Evaluate final efforts to *prove* learning
Timing: During the learning segment	Timing: At the end of the learning segment
Informal teacher questions	Formal oral interview
Conversation with student	Conference with student
Informal observation	Formal observation
Rough drafts of written work	Final copy of written work
Learning log (in progress)	Final learning log entries
Reflective journal (multiple drafts)	Final journal entries
Mathematics problem solving steps	Mathematics final solution
Practice science experiment	Final science experiment
Rehearsal of presentation	Final presentation
Working portfolio	Showcase portfolio
Practice checklist for do-overs	Final checklist
Practice rubrics (analytical)	Final rubrics (analytical and holistic)
Homework, quizzes	Teacher-made tests
Benchmark/interim tests	High-stakes standardized tests

Note: The language of the standards is embedded in all formative and summative assessments.

Final Thoughts

The title of this chapter is "The Balanced Assessment Model: When Formative Meets Summative." Some educators seem to believe that the subtitle should be "Formative Versus Summative Assessment." There's almost an either/or competition rather than a both/and collaboration. National conferences advertise they are focusing on "assessment *of* learning" or "assessment *for* learning" as if the two were competing with each other.

Lee Shulman (1988) called assessment a "union of insufficiencies" because he realized that no one or two assessment tools could ever provide a true portrait of a learner. Teachers who draw upon a rich repertoire of both formative and summative assessment strategies capture the strengths, weaknesses, interests, styles, and motivation levels of their learners. They know that balanced assessment is effective assessment. As Huebner (2009, p. 87) puts it, "a well-planned approach to balanced assessment will offer teachers, principals, and superintendents the different kinds of data they need to be well-informed decision makers." The purpose and the timing of an assessment determine whether it should be categorized as either formative or summative, and they are both good things!

Concluding Exercises

Reflections on the Balanced Assessment Model

1 How would you self-assess your assessment literacy quotient?

2 Why has feedback been described as the "heart and soul" of formative assessment?

3 Describe how corrective interventions are related to differentiated teaching strategies and response to intervention (RTI).

4 How do the *purpose* of the assessment and the *timing* of the assessment determine its classification as either formative or summative?

5 How do your formative assessments provide constructive feedback and result in valid summative grades?

Action Steps

List three action steps you plan to take to balance your assessments.

Step 1:

Step 2:

Step 3:

3

Common Assessments: A Community of Assessors

The sheer number of standards and the challenge of creating valid and reliable assessments to measure them preclude the traditional model of teachers working in isolation. Teachers today need to work in teams to create quality common assessments based on the standards to ensure consistency and equity for all their students.

What Are Common Assessments?

Common assessments are formative or summative assessments that are designed by a grade-level, departmental, or vertical team, or by a district, for the purpose of assessing multiple groups of students throughout a school or district. They usually are created by teams of teachers who teach the same class or grade level. Often, they are used as school-level assessments to provide evidence to teacher leaders, curriculum personnel, and administrators that students throughout the school are meeting the standards. The data from the assessments help educators know what is working and what needs more work (Stiggins & DuFour, 2009). Common assessments are often created across a school district to ensure consistency and equity. Stiggins and DuFour (2009) refer to "institutional-level assessments"—common assessments that serve summative purposes to find out if schools and districts are as effective as they should be.

Common formative assessments require teachers to meet and agree on what they plan to teach, what they plan to assess, and how they plan to assess it. According to Young (2009, p. 135), "common formative assessments demand discussion about the best ways to help students learn the agreed-upon outcomes. They require consensus regarding the best way for students to demonstrate their learning." Common assessments show teachers where they have to make adjustments in their teaching to meet the diverse needs of their students. They also ensure some consistency across all subject areas and grade levels.

Common assessments usually focus on important standards, sometimes called power standards, that are aligned to large-scale assessments. Once the teams develop common formative assessments, teachers use them periodically throughout the year to assess student understanding of specific standards. Formative assessment informs instruction and predicts the results students are likely to achieve on large-scale summative assessments. When teachers receive the results of the common "practice" assessments, they use the data to adjust their instruction so that students both deepen their understanding of key concepts and are better prepared to take the large-scale and often high-stakes assessments. Ainsworth and Viegut (2006, p. 3) note that

> in understanding the role formative assessments play in an interdependent instruction and assessment system, educators come to realize how all the pieces fit together into one cohesive and powerful whole. In glimpsing the potential impact this practice can have on advancing all students to proficiency and beyond, teachers *make time* for this powerful practice.

Why Should Teachers Work in Collaborative Teams to Create Common Assessments?

Stiggins and DuFour (2009) believe that one of the most powerful ways to redefine the role of assessment in school improvement is to form professional learning communities (PLCs) to create common assessments. In order to promote both student and teacher success, the formative assessments must contribute to productive instructional decision making, and they must be high quality. Most importantly, the rigorous common assessments must improve student learning. Stiggins and DuFour (2009, p. 641) explain that

> in professional learning communities, collaborative teams of teachers create common assessments for three formative purposes. First, team-developed common assessments help identify curricular areas that need attention because many students are struggling. Second, they help each team member clarify strengths and weaknesses in his or her teaching and create a forum for teachers to learn from one another. Third, interim common assessments identify students who aren't mastering the intended standards and need timely and systematic interventions.

Of course, even the most collaborative common assessments will not be valid unless they measure what they were supposed to measure. As discussed in chapter 1, teacher teams must target state standards and district curriculum goals by deconstructing the concepts, big ideas, essential questions, and the language of the standards (LOTS). Then they create effective assessments that transform the learning target into learning progressions for all students to learn at higher levels.

What Is a Common Assessment Cycle?

There are many effective methods of creating common assessments. Figure 3.1 illustrates one possible format for a common assessment cycle that has been successful in schools and districts. The remainder of this chapter will describe each step in detail.

Step 1

Identify the power standards in all content areas, K–12.

Step 2

Repack the standards and target the big ideas and LOTS (language of the standards).

Step 3

Write test-bank questions to assess knowledge and skills that can be judged objectively.

Step 4

Create performance tasks, checklists, and rubrics to assess work that requires subjective judgments.

Step 5

Teach the standards and use diagnostic and formative assessments to provide feedback.

Step 6

Examine student work and analyze data to determine what needs more work.

Step 7

Differentiate instruction and use additional formative assessments to provide specific feedback targeted to the standards.

Step 8

Administer and evaluate summative assessments and assign final course grades.

Figure 3.1: A common assessment cycle.

Step 1: Identify the Power Standards

The "less is more" philosophy has not been widely adopted by committees writing state standards. As mentioned in chapter 1, Marzano has found that the sheer number of standards is the biggest impediment to implementing them, and he recommends cutting two-thirds of the content to be able to cover them in depth (Scherer, 2001). However, many teachers don't feel comfortable de-emphasizing or deleting standards on their own. Cutting content, therefore, is not an option for most educators. If the standards are important, teachers must be given enough time not only to teach them but also to have students apply their knowledge of the standards to real-life tasks or performances. Moreover, teachers need time to *assess* students' understanding of the important concepts.

Content standards can be assessed with paper-and-pencil tests that use a combination of selected-response (true/false, fill-in-the-blank, multiple-choice) questions and that may take less time to grade. Most states, however, use performance standards to focus on students' ability to apply their factual knowledge and skills to an authentic task. Asking students to name the five parts of a business letter requires much less time than having students *write* a business letter. It is difficult to assess most performance tasks using a paper-and-pencil test. Since performance tasks address multiple criteria and are judged more subjectively, teachers need to use checklists or rubrics to assess them. Performance assessments, by their nature, require more time to develop, administer, and assess.

Reeves' (2003) idea of determining power standards based on the criteria of endurance, leverage, and necessity for the next level of instruction, as described in chapter 1, helps teacher teams review all their standards in each grade level and subject area and select the key standards. For example, persuasive writing is a power standard because it *endures* through elementary, middle school, high school, college, and life; it has *leverage* because it can be applied in multiple academic disciplines; it is *necessary for the next level of instruction* because students will build on their skills; and it is often mandated on high-stakes state writing tests for all students. Similarly, standards like informational reading and writing, mathematical relationships, scientific inquiry, oral communication, and thinking skills are threaded throughout multiple courses and grade levels.

Ainsworth and Viegut (2006) recommend that teacher teams identify the power standards for each individual grade and course and then create a curriculum map to determine when each standard will be taught and when it will be assessed. Jacobs (1997) first discussed curriculum mapping as a way to find out what teachers are teaching in what grade levels and to discover any gaps within one school or among schools in a district. She says, "To make sense of our students' experiences over time, we need two lenses: a zoom lens into this year's curriculum for a particular grade and a wide-angle lens to see the K–12 perspective. The classroom (or micro) level is dependent on the site and district level (a macro view)" (p. 3). The vertical alignment ensures that the standards will be taught in a logical and developmentally appropriate sequence beginning in kindergarten and culminating in grade 12. The power standards can be emphasized to remind educators of their importance. Ainsworth and Viegut (2006, p. 32) note that

> Power Standards are not a license to eliminate—and thus fail to teach—standards that have not been so designated. Even though individual educators will teach and assess *both* the Power Standards and the non-Power Standards in their respective grades and courses, common formative assessments are principally designed to provide teachers with information about how their students are progressing towards the understanding of the Power Standards.

In addition to identifying the power standards, teams of teachers must focus on preparing students for the high-stakes state tests. Most states provide an analysis of approximately how many questions on these tests focus on specific standards. Districts and schools examine data that dig deeper into how many questions address a concept or indicator, as well as how many questions students answered correctly or incorrectly on past tests. Teams of teachers need to take these data into consideration when they select the power standards.

Creating checklists and rubrics is a demanding and time-consuming process. It is almost impossible to create a valid and reliable assessment for each standard. By focusing on the power standards, teachers prioritize their teaching and focus on what is most important for students.

Step 2: Repack the Standards

As mentioned in chapter 1, standards are not always written in user-friendly language. Repacking the standards can make them easier to use. After analyzing the various elements of the standards and clustering them appropriately, teachers can create lesson plans describing where to start their instruction, what to cover, and where to end.

To repack a middle school math standard for "Data Analysis and Probability," one team of teachers reviewed the standard and then chunked all the performance indicators into five major categories:

1   Pose questions.
2   Collect data.
3   Represent data.
4   Analyze data.
5   Use appropriate graphs to analyze data.

After they determined the big chunks, the two teachers who made up the team worked together to identify which specific subskills belonged under each one. Then they put the repacked standard into a checklist format (fig. 3.2, page 32). This checklist included columns for each quarter of the school year so that the teachers would be able to keep track of when they introduced each performance indicator and make sure they were following the scope and sequence for the course. Since this was a power standard, it would thread throughout other standards and be reinforced in subsequent lessons, courses, and years of mathematics. The teachers could decide to spend more time on particular indicators if their students needed more intensive instruction, and they could differentiate their teaching methods to meet the needs of their diverse learners. But both team members knew their target goals and used the checklist as a roadmap to guide their instruction and assessment.

The teachers also extracted the vocabulary from the standards and included it at the end of their checklist. They would then be able to use the terminology to create an informal oral or written diagnostic assessment to determine the prior knowledge of their students. The assessment data would help guide their instruction throughout the year.

Data Analysis and Probability Checklist

Standard: Students will pose questions, collect data, represent and analyze data, and interpret results.

The students will:	1st 9 weeks	2nd 9 weeks	3rd 9 weeks	4th 9 weeks
Pose questions				
• Formulate questions				
• Ask questions				
Collect data				
• Collect data from a census of at least 30 objects				
• Collect data from samples of varying sizes				
Represent data by constructing:				
• Frequency distributions				
• Pictographs				
• Histograms				
• Bar graphs				
• Line graphs				
• Circle graphs				
• Line plots				
• Box-and-whisker plots				
• Scatter plots				

Figure 3.2: Checklist for repacked "Data Analysis and Probability" standard.

	1st 9 weeks	2nd 9 weeks	3rd 9 weeks	4th 9 weeks
Analyze data				
• Analyze data using measures of central tendency (mean, median, and mode)				
• Analyze data using measures of variation (range, quartiles, inter-quartile range)				
• Compare measures of central tendency and variation from samples to those of a census				
• Analyze and draw conclusions including the relationship between two variables				
Analyze data using appropriate graphs				
• Pictographs				
• Histograms				
• Bar graphs				
• Line graphs				
• Circle graphs				
• Line plots				
• Box-and-whisker plots				
• Scatter plots				
Vocabulary				
Mean				
Median				
Mode				

continued on next page →

	1st 9 weeks	2nd 9 weeks	3rd 9 weeks	4th 9 weeks
Range				
Quartile				
Inter-quartile range				
Outlier				
Histogram				
Scatter plot				
Line plot				
Plot				
Box-and-whisker plot				
Variation				

Created by Patti Allen and Matilda Strickland; Carrollton Junior High; Carrollton City Schools; Carrollton, Georgia. Used with permission.

Step 3: Write Test-Bank Questions

Many districts administer interim assessments—also known as benchmark assessments, periodic tests, or short-cycle assessments—every four to nine weeks to check their students' progress. According to Marshall (2008, p. 64), these periodic tests lead teachers to realize that "initial teaching, no matter how good, can't bring all students to proficiency because of differences in their prior knowledge, attention, and motivation." Moreover, when tests are administered at the end of the year, it is too late to discover who does not understand the material. It is better to remediate learning problems early in the year and throughout the year, before the students are too far behind to attain proficiency.

When teachers don't use some type of interim assessment, the achievement gap widens. Unfortunately, as Marshall (2008, p. 65) relates, this is a very common state of affairs, resulting in inequality in schools: "The students who enter with disadvantages tend to be the same ones who don't understand after initial teaching, and they are also the ones who are harmed most when teachers move on without checking for understanding and following up. The rich get richer and the poor get poorer." Minute-to-minute formative assessments used throughout each lesson provide the most useful feedback to target confused students quickly. But informal or formal benchmark tests administered once or twice a quarter should also identify struggling students and allow enough time for interventions before the final test.

Often, districts will purchase benchmark tests from publishing companies that specialize in producing and selling state-specific test-preparation materials. Some districts or schools create their own test bank of questions correlated to their curriculum and the state standards. Even if a district purchases interim tests, it is important for teachers to develop original test questions to use in their classes. Using the language of their state standards as well as vocabulary from the school's curriculum, teams of teachers should write some common selected-response test items—that is, multiple-choice, true/false, and matching questions, which have predetermined responses from which students can choose. Teachers who write benchmark test questions as common assessments improve their own instruction as well as prepare students for standardized tests.

Gareis and Grant (2008) note that writing test items that address both the content and the level of cognitive demand of the standards is challenging. Multiple-choice items are not typically considered appropriate for assessing higher cognitive levels, although it is possible to write them in such a way that they fulfill this function. Supply-response or constructed-response items—questions to which students provide the answers themselves—allow teachers to assess a range of cognitive levels. Supply-response items include fill-in-the-blank (or completion), short-answer, and essay questions. Gareis and Grant (2008, p. 127) classify performances, projects, and original creations as supply-response assessment items, but they say, "These types of assessments do not lend themselves to paper-and-pencil tests and are usually conducted as part of an overall assessment plan that may include paper-and-pencil tests *and* projects, performance assessments, or original creations." Performances and projects are usually assessed by checklists or rubrics, which are covered in step 4.

Step 4: Create Student Checklists and Rubrics

Power standards for performance tasks usually integrate content standards with multiple process standards. Such standards meet Reeves' (2003) criterion of "leverage" because they apply to more than one discipline. For example, science students could be assigned to write a persuasive essay arguing a position on global warming. They would demonstrate their content knowledge by using science vocabulary, quoting scientists, and basing their arguments on facts and statistics from scientific research. They would also have to demonstrate their ability to write a persuasive essay, which requires knowledge of the writing process; understanding of grammar, usage, and conventions; and research and technology skills.

The language of the process standard provides the essential framework for writing a persuasive essay, but, as discussed earlier, teachers can help students make sense of the standard's terminology by creating a common assessment in the form of a checklist. The checklist serves as an instructional tool to guide both teachers and students through the multistep process of writing the persuasive essay, as well as an assessment tool to determine students' progress toward meeting the writing standard. Checklists used for assessment are not usually graded, because they are formative in nature, but they do provide specific feedback to guide future instruction and showcase the need for differentiated instruction or interventions.

In chapter 1, teachers worked as a team to create a common assessment checklist that they would use to teach the persuasive essay to their fourth- and fifth-grade students and to assess their students' progress as they completed each step of the process. Because producing a persuasive essay is a power standard that threads through all grade levels, seventh-grade teachers in the same school system also worked as a team to create a checklist they would use to teach the essay process, assess their students' ability to complete each step, and allow students to work at their own pace and self-assess their progress. The seventh-grade teachers used some of the same criteria that the fourth- and fifth-grade team had used, but they included additional indicators to require a higher level of writing from their students. They made the process of writing a persuasive essay even more concrete by breaking down each paragraph of a five-paragraph essay into specific steps.

Figure 3.3 shows the seventh-grade common assessment checklist for the persuasive essay standard. The specific language of the standard appears in boldface capital letters to draw attention to the key vocabulary embedded in the standard and its indicators. The columns on the right of the checklist labeled "Not Yet" and "Yes" ask both teachers and students to assess whether the indicators have been met or still need to be met. The checklist also has some blanks for students to fill in with answers to specific questions about their work so that teachers can quickly assess whether or not they are on the right track. If the teachers see that some students do not understand the process, they can intervene immediately to help them before they complete the entire essay incorrectly. Some students tend to check things off without really doing them, so the questions and blanks require them to write something before checking off "yes" on the right.

Even though most teachers do not give grades on formative assessments, students need to know what score they would have received if this checklist had been graded. The score is a prediction of how they might do on the final summative assessment, which will be graded. Thus the right-hand columns also indicate that a student receives one point for each indicator checked in the "yes" column, and the points are totaled at the bottom.

During step 4, the seventh-grade teacher team also created a rubric that was an extension of the checklist. The rubric lists the same criteria for writing the persuasive essay, but it provides more descriptors of quality work and will lead to the final summative grade once the formative process ends. Checklists and rubrics will be discussed in more detail in chapters 5 and 6.

Textbooks may provide a unit on the persuasive essay along with checklists and rubrics, but unless the textbook was published expressly for a particular state, the language could be different. Common assessments created by a team of teachers using the exact language of their state standards are more valuable teaching tools and are probably more valid than many textbook assessments or benchmark assessments created by publishing companies.

Persuasive Essay Checklist

Standard: English language arts, grade 7: The student demonstrates competence in a variety of genres.

Performance Indicators	Not Yet 0	Yes 1
INTRODUCTORY PARAGRAPH		
A. Does my writing **ENGAGE THE READER**?		
1. Is my **PURPOSE** in writing clear? (to persuade)		
2. Do I create a "**SPEAKER'S VOICE**"?		
3. Do I use one of the following strategies to **DEVELOP READER INTEREST**? (Circle the strategy used and write your example in box.) —Question —Startling fact —Scenario —Dazzling description —Anecdote —Quote		
B. Do I state a **CLEAR POSITION OR PERSPECTIVE** in support of my proposition or proposal?		
1. Is the **PROBLEM** clear to the reader?		
2. Is my **OPINION** clear to the reader?		
3. Do I have a clearly developed **THESIS STATEMENT**?		
BODY PARAGRAPH 1		
C. Does my paragraph begin with a **TRANSITIONAL WORD, PHRASE,** or **SENTENCE**? Write it: _____		

Figure 3.3: Common assessment checklist for grade-7 persuasive essay.

continued on next page →

	Not Yet 0	Yes 1
D. Does the paragraph have a clear **TOPIC SENTENCE**?		
E. Does the paragraph **SUPPORT FIRST MAIN POINT** of the thesis?		
F. Do I anticipate **READERS' CONCERNS** and/or **COUNTERARGUMENTS**? How? _____		
G. Do I provide **SUPPORT FOR MY OPINION**?		
1. Do I use **WELL-ARTICULATED EVIDENCE**? (Circle the strategy used and write your example in box.) —Logical arguments —Statistics —Expert opinions —Personal observations —Charged (emotional) language —Striking images		
2. Are all of my supporting details **RELEVANT** to my argument? —Do I exclude irrelevant facts, statistics, and arguments?		
3. Does my paragraph end with a **CLINCHER SENTENCE** that supports the argument of body paragraph 1?		
BODY PARAGRAPH 2		
H. Does my paragraph begin with a **TRANSITIONAL WORD, PHRASE,** or **SENTENCE**? Write it: _____		
I. Does the paragraph have a clear **TOPIC SENTENCE**?		
J. Does the paragraph **SUPPORT SECOND MAIN POINT** of the thesis?		

	Not Yet 0	Yes 1
K. Do I anticipate **READERS' CONCERNS** and/or **COUNTERARGUMENTS**?		
L. Do I provide **SUPPORT FOR MY OPINION**?		
1. Do I use **WELL-ARTICULATED EVIDENCE**? (Circle the strategy used and write your example in box.) —Logical arguments —Statistics —Expert opinions —Personal observations —Charged (emotional) language —Striking images		
2. Are all of my supporting details **RELEVANT** to my argument? —Do I exclude irrelevant facts, statistics, and arguments?		
3. Do I correctly **CITE** researched ideas to avoid plagiarism?		
M. Does my paragraph end with a **CLINCHER SENTENCE** that supports the argument of body paragraph 2? What is it? _____		
BODY PARAGRAPH 3		
N. Does my paragraph begin with a **TRANSITIONAL WORD, PHRASE,** or **SENTENCE**? Write it: _____		
O. Does the paragraph have a clear **TOPIC SENTENCE**?		
P. Does the paragraph **SUPPORT THIRD MAIN POINT** of the thesis?		
Q. Do I anticipate **READERS' CONCERNS** and/or **COUNTERARGUMENTS**?		

continued on next page →

	Not Yet 0	Yes 1
R. Do I provide **SUPPORT FOR MY OPINION**?		
1. Do I use **WELL-ARTICULATED EVIDENCE**? (Circle the strategy used and write your example in box.) —Logical arguments —Statistics —Expert opinions —Personal observations —Charged (emotional) language —Striking images		
2. Are all of my supporting details **RELEVANT** to my argument? —Do I exclude irrelevant facts, statistics, and arguments?		
3. Do I correctly **CITE** researched ideas to avoid plagiarism?		
S. Does my paragraph end with a **CLINCHER SENTENCE** that supports the argument of body paragraph 3? Write it: _____		
CONCLUDING PARAGRAPH		
T. Does my paragraph begin with a **TRANSITIONAL WORD, PHRASE,** or **SENTENCE**? Write it: _____		
U. Does my writing provide a **SENSE OF CLOSURE?**		
1. Do I **SUMMARIZE** my arguments?		
2. Do I **RESTATE** my thesis?		
3. Do I **CLOSE** with one of the following? (Circle the strategy used and write your example in box.) —Call to action/recommendation —Memorable image —Brief story —Question —Prediction —Phrase/quote		

	Not Yet 0	Yes 1
MISCELLANEOUS		
V. Have I incorporated **DIRECT QUOTATIONS**?		
1. Did I use **THREE** direct quotations?		
2. Have I correctly **PUNCTUATED** the quotations? (quotation marks, commas, end marks)		
3. Have I **CITED** the quotations correctly?		
W. Does my essay contain an accurately formatted **BIBLIOGRAPHY**?		
1. Do I have at least **THREE SOURCES**?		
2. Are all sources in my bibliography **REFERENCED IN THE ESSAY**?		
3. Have I completed the **BIBLIOGRAPHY CHECKLIST** to ensure that I follow all rules of format?		
TOTAL POINTS		

Signature of Writer: _____

Comments:

Signature of Conference Partner: _____

Comments:

Scale

42–47 = Exceeds Standards

38–41 = Meets Standards

33–37 = In Progress

0–32 = Novice

Created by John Megathlin, Kisha Mitchell, Amy Mulvehill, and Camille P. Sanders; Carrollton Junior High School; Carrollton City Schools; Carrollton, Georgia. Used with permission.

Step 5: Teach the Standard and Use Formative Assessments

In step 5, teachers select appropriate instructional strategies to teach each chunk of the standard. The instructional strategies could include worksheets and drills, reviewing chapters in a textbook, or more "authentic" approaches. Teachers who use a repertoire of different strategies that target different types of learning will engage more students in the process. Table 3.1 (page 42) lists a variety of learning experiences that are classified according to the multiple intelligences first described by Howard Gardner (1983/1993) in his book *Frames of Mind: The Theory of Multiple Intelligences*.

Table 3.1: Learning Experiences Classified by Gardner's Multiple Intelligences

Verbal/ Linguistic	Logical/ Mathematical	Visual/ Spatial	Bodily/ Kinesthetic
Logs, journals	Puzzles	Artwork	Field trips
Speeches	Outlines	Photographs	Role playing
Debates	Timelines	Math manipulatives	Learning centers
Storytelling	Analogies	Graphic organizers	Labs
Reports	Patterns	Posters, charts	Sports, games
Crosswords	Problem solving	Illustrations	Cooperative learning
Newspapers	Lab experiments	Cartoons	Body language
Internet sites	Formulas	Props for plays	Experiments
Books		Use of projector	Performance tasks

Musical/ Rhythmic	Interpersonal	Intrapersonal	Naturalist
Background music	Group video, film, slides	Reflective journals	Outdoor education
Songs about books, people, countries, historic events	Team computer programs	Learning logs	Environmental studies
Raps	Think-pair-share	Goal-setting journals	Field trips (farm, zoo)
Jingles	Cooperative tasks	Metacognitive reflections	Bird watching
Choirs	Jigsaws	Independent reading	Nature walk
	Conferences	Silent reflection	Weather forecasting
	Interviews	Diaries	Stargazing
	Peer tutoring	Processing pieces	Exploring nature
			Ecology studies
			Leaf identification
			Science experiments

Source: Burke, K. (2009). *How to assess authentic learning* (5th ed.). Thousand Oaks, CA: Corwin Press. Reprinted by permission.

The second part of step 5 is conducting formative assessments. In practice, formative assessment does not have to be formal or lengthy. It can be a short activity designed to give meaningful feedback to teachers to improve their instruction. It also provides feedback to students to improve their academic achievement. As Reeves (2009, p. 91) says, "Tests designed only to render an evaluation cannot achieve the potential of assessment for learning that assessment experts have suggested is an essential element of effective practice."

According to Wiliam and Leahy and Wiliam and Thompson (cited in Wiliam, 2007, p. 192), effective formative assessment consists of five key strategies:

1 Clarifying learning intentions and sharing criteria for success

2 Engineering effective classroom discussions, questions, and learning tasks that elicit evidence of learning

3 Providing feedback that moves learners forward

4 Activating students as the owners of their own learning

5 Activating students as instructional resources for one another

Marshall (2008) agrees with Paul Black and Dylan Wiliam's finding, reported in their 1998 study "Inside the Black Box," that informal, moment-to-moment assessments are quick and powerful, and if used within twenty-four hours of the initial teaching can significantly improve students' long-term memory. Marshall (2008, p. 66) notes, "If teachers find out immediately which students don't understand and which concepts are not getting through, they can clarify and re-teach before misconceptions and misunderstandings widen the achievement gap, and they can use the insights to teach the concept more effectively the next time around." There are many options for quick, informal assessments. For example, students can write on small whiteboards and hold them up so that teachers can see if they understand a question. Students can hold up a green cup or card if they are clear on a concept and a red cup or card if they need to stop and clarify something. Teachers can give pop quizzes. Students can give ticket-out-the-door exit cards to the teacher to share what they have learned or what questions they have. Teachers can randomly call on students using name cards drawn from a box. Or teachers can use effective questioning, checklists, or practice problems to see where students are stuck in a process. Chapter 7 will present other possibilities for informal assessments.

Step 6: Examine Student Work

After teachers assign students a task and assess the results using the checklist and rubric, they meet in collaborative teams to examine student work. In these meetings, teachers reflect on what they have learned about their students and discuss their common goals. They discuss how to change their curriculum or instruction. They can make decisions about how to differentiate instruction to meet goals, and they can focus on one or two questions by concentrating on a particular aspect of the performance tasks.

Hord and Sommers (2008, p. 34) believe that collaboration is important but collegiality is even more important. They define *collegiality* as "collaborating plus sharing information and feedback. Collegiality is learning and working together and toward a common purpose. Collegiality is giving and accepting feedback, which makes us better practitioners." Teachers who engage in collegiality share their repertoire of strategies with one another. This is how group wisdom gets transferred throughout the organization. According to Blythe, Allen, and Powell (2008, pp. 11–12), some common purposes for examining and discussing student work include the following:

- Learning more about an individual child's response to an assignment
- Setting standards for all students' performances
- Learning about your own teaching and assessment practices
- Honing observational and interpretive skills, which can be used in the classroom as well as within protocols
- Developing a common language or criteria for discussing teaching and learning

Easton (2009) recommends establishing a *protocol,* an agreed-upon set of guidelines for conversation. She describes a protocol as a code of behavior or a *modus operandi* for groups to use when exploring ideas. She says, "By following accepted parameters for conversation, group members can have very focused conversations. Protocols help educators look at student work, artifacts or educator practice, texts relating to education, or problems and issues that surface during educators' day-to-day lives" (p. 1). When teams use protocols, teachers feel more comfortable creating and reviewing lessons together, observing one another teaching, offering one another feedback, and assisting in selecting and developing curriculum units and assessments.

The teachers who collaboratively developed the checklist and rubric as a common assessment for the persuasive writing standard are more likely to offer suggestions and resources to other teachers to help them develop lessons to teach student writers such skills as how to engage their readers. They might share sample hooks or motivators, stem starters, examples of famous first lines in stories, or student examples. A teacher who has successfully taught engagement in writing should be willing to share his or her good ideas with the team, with the expectation that at the next session someone else will share ideas about mastering another aspect of the standard—perhaps how to write an effective thesis statement with three controlling ideas. Reciprocity is one of the keys to collegiality.

Step 7: Differentiate Instruction

When the assessment shows that students did not "get it," teachers can change their teaching strategies by differentiating their instruction. All students have the capacity to meet the standards and be successful in school. Hierck (2009, p. 249) points out:

As educators, it is our job to unlock the potential in all of our learners, particularly our most challenging ones, and point them in the direction most likely to produce the greatest chance for success. What qualifies as success will vary for individual students—education is a very personal journey—and will require from us a differentiated approach to instruction based on assessment data.

Differentiated learning requires teachers to "change something" in their instructional input. Tomlinson and Eidson (2003) address five classroom elements teachers can modify or differentiate in order to improve student learning: content, process, product, affect, and learning environment.

One way to change the content is by changing the *complexity*: using three tiers of learning ranging from the concrete level to the symbolic level to the highest level—abstract. Fogarty (2001) gives the example of a lesson on magnets. At the concrete level, students could work with magnets and objects to engage in a hands-on investigation. At the symbolic level, students could view a video about magnets and then draw scientific diagrams depicting the direction of the magnetic fields in various instances.

At the abstract level, students could read the textbook, hear a lecture, and then discuss the concept of gravitational pull.

Another way teachers can change the content is to change the *resources*. Instead of having all the students read a chapter about the 1920s in their textbook, the teacher could give students the option of reading the novel *The Great Gatsby*, seeing the film, or reading a biography of Zelda Fitzgerald.

In addition to changing the content, teachers can change the *process* of teaching and learning. Instead of relying solely on direct instruction, a teacher could have students work in cooperative groups or inquiry groups to make sense of key ideas using essential skills. The teacher could also use flexible groupings based on readiness, interests, or learning profiles to meet students' diverse needs (Tomlinson & Eidson, 2003).

In order to change the *product*, teachers can allow students to demonstrate what they have learned through different assessment formats (posters, skits, multimedia presentations, simulation games) that appeal to students' interests and their levels of readiness and motivation.

Allowing students to select topics that they feel strongly about will help them link the cognitive domain with the affective domain. If students select a topic like cancer to research because one of their family members is undergoing treatment, the *affect* will engage them more deeply.

Finally, teachers can change the *learning environment* by finding different ways to use time, space, or materials in the classroom or by taking the students outside the classroom to go on a field trip, take a nature walk, or work on a community project.

Teachers develop a repertoire of teaching and assessment strategies that help one student, a small group of students, or the whole class meet the standards. Working in teacher teams throughout the common assessment process helps establish a community of learners who share instructional strategies with one another. The essence of job-embedded professional development is the *moment-to-moment* advice from fellow teachers. A colleague might suggest a book or film to use in a unit. During a team meeting, a teacher might demonstrate an effective graphic organizer or engaging instructional technique he or she used to teach a concept. Teachers can observe one another's classes and conduct mini-lesson demonstrations during their planning periods. Since the teacher teams are covering the same standards, addressing the same curriculum, and implementing the same common assessments, they are all working together toward a common goal.

Step 8: Administer Summative Assessment

As explained in chapter 2, the purpose and the timing of an assessment determine whether it is classified as formative or summative. If the purpose is to provide ongoing feedback to improve learning, the assessment is probably formative. If the purpose is to make a final judgment after the assessment information has been collected, synthesized, and thought about, the assessment is probably summative (Airasian, 2000). If the assessment is administered early in the grading period when a new concept has just been introduced, it is probably formative in nature. If the assessment is administered at the end of a learning period or grading period, it is probably summative in nature.

If teachers began with the end in mind, then the same common formative assessment used to provide feedback to students and teachers can be administered as the final common summative assessment. The standards, indicators, criteria, and language of the standards remain the same. But now the practice period, the do-overs, and the moment-to-moment feedback loop are over. The summative assessment provides the last piece of measurement data necessary for the teacher to make a final evaluation of the student. The feedback goes from being descriptive to being more succinct: pass/fail, graduation/summer school, A-B-C-D-F. This is the "last hurrah" in the classroom assessment cycle. The final summative assessment will not be able to help the current student improve, but it will help teachers make some changes in their teaching for next year's students.

Many common summative assessments resemble assessments on large-scale standardized tests because they are developed from the standards and target power standards. Teachers have the dual goals of helping students achieve deep understanding of important standards and helping them to score high on mandated high-stakes tests (assessments *of* learning) that determine promotion/retention, scholarships, membership in honor societies, school probations or awards, and funding.

Final Thoughts

The eight steps of the common assessment cycle presented in this chapter may seem daunting at first, but teachers will be surprised to learn how many of the steps they are already doing in their schools or district. The process involves several best practices in education that may have different labels but are basically targeting the same purposes. Some of these practices include the following:

Collaboration

- Professional learning communities (PLCs)
- Vertical teaming
- Curriculum-mapping teams
- Data teams
- Grade-level teams
- Subject-area teams
- Job-embedded professional development
- Common assessment teams

Instruction

- Curriculum units correlated to the standards
- Cooperative learning
- Inquiry models of instruction
- Independent learning
- Differentiated instruction
- Flexible groupings
- Learning experiences based on multiple intelligences
- Response to intervention
- Standards-based teaching

Assessment

- Diagnostic testing
- Standards-based assessments
- Formative assessments
- Benchmark/interim/short-cycle assessments
- Checklists/rubrics
- Selected-response test questions
- Constructed-response test questions
- Examining student work
- Portfolios
- Summative assessments
- High-stakes standardized tests

It is clear that many of the components necessary for creating standards-based common assessments are already in place in many schools. The key is organizing teacher talent to maximize the results.

Concluding Exercises

Reflections on Common Assessments

1 How do teachers in your school or district collaborate?

2 Why do standards play such a critical role in the development of common assessments?

3 How does job-embedded professional development at the school level improve student learning?

4 Why should schools use benchmark, interim, or short-cycle formative common assessments throughout the year?

5 How can teachers differentiate their instruction to meet the diverse needs of all their students?

Action Steps

List three action steps you plan to take with a team to create common assessments.

Step 1:

Step 2:

Step 3:

4

Performance Tasks: The Key to an Engaging Curriculum

Much of the curriculum covered in schools is derived from state standards, textbooks, school goals, educational outcomes, and learning objectives. Educators do not have much choice about what material they have to teach, but they do have a choice about how to structure the information to motivate students and engage them more fully in their own learning.

What Is Wrong With the Curriculum?

Meeting or exceeding standards may be an important goal of education in today's results-driven environment, but many students don't have the patience or the self-discipline to endure thirteen years of school for the purpose of passing tests. Regardless of the need to meet standards, take practice benchmark tests, and pass high-stakes state tests or end-of-course tests, most students demand and deserve more in the classroom. Darling-Hammond (2009) believes that teachers must be knowledge-able about how to teach diverse students and must continuously build on their pedagogical knowledge base. Then, she believes, teams of teachers have to work on the curriculum. "How," she asks, "can we get the standards conceptualized in a way that is leaner, as other countries do, so we can teach deeply, using a project-based curriculum organized around those standards?" She suggests that "we have to transform the curriculum so [students] really care about it, so it's meaningful to them, so they're doing the kinds of exhibitions and demonstrations of learning that motivate them" (2009, p. 53).

Research shows that most children begin life ready and willing to learn. But as they progress through elementary school, many of them lose their natural curiosity and enthusiasm for learning. What has happened to cause so many children and young adults to question why they have to learn something? Moreover, what has happened to cause so many students to decide that what they are studying is not important and that they would be better off dropping out of school? The report *The Silent Epidemic: Perspectives of High School Dropouts,* published in 2006, notes that the graduation rate in America is "between 68 and 71 percent, which means that almost one-third of all public high school students fail to graduate. . . . The rate at which [minority students] finish public high school with a regular diploma declines to approximately 50 percent" (Bridgeland, Dilulio, & Morison, 2006, p. 1).

Schools are losing young people to the streets before they graduate because they have lost interest in school. Kids today are not going to sit quietly in their seats and complete worksheets and test-prep materials if these activities are not meaningful to them. Many students are not motivated by extrinsic rewards such as passing state tests, nor are they threatened by sanctions such as attending summer school or repeating a grade or course. They are captivated by technology, fast-paced television shows, movies and interactive videos, YouTube, Twitter, Facebook, and other social networks that interest them far more than the Articles of Confederation or possessive pronouns. Teachers cannot compete with the communication and entertainment industries, but they need to try to make learning more authentic and interactive. If teachers transformed traditional standards-based lessons into fascinating learning experiences, more students would engage more fully in their own learning.

Schmoker (2009) maintains that simple, fundamental changes in instruction could make huge differences in student learning. Rather than using worksheets, showing movies, or having students create collages, construct mobiles, or build medieval castles, teachers need to teach an agreed-on curriculum that includes higher-order literacy and problem solving. Schmoker believes that "if we replaced the most egregious and time-wasting activities with vastly more reading, writing, and discussion, something marvelous would happen for students" (p. 525). He also notes that true professional learning communities (PLCs) give teams time to meet regularly to build curriculum-based lessons and units that target higher-order skills and habits of mind. He says, "Authentic teams build effective curriculum-based lessons and units together—which they routinely refine together on the basis of common assessment data" (p. 527). The teams create authentic and engaging learning experiences that captivate their students while addressing the standards.

Who Designs the Curriculum?

The introduction of accountability measures made districts realize that standards alone could not increase student achievement. According to Moody and Stricker (2009), many districts reacted to this situation by buying scripted curriculum programs from publishers. These programs were loaded with ancillary materials such as PowerPoint presentations and test banks of questions. When districts shifted from instructor-designed curriculum to prepackaged programs and students still did not succeed, educators blamed the publishers for ineffective programs, and publishers blamed the teachers for ineffective implementation. District personnel would then purchase another prescriptive program, and teachers would become frustrated because they had to learn yet another one. Unfortunately, this cycle repeats itself so often that many teachers become cynical about education reform. They resent the newest "research-based, best-practices, data-driven, results-based curriculum program." Arthur Costa, an international author and consultant, once asked educators in a workshop, "How many back-to-basic programs have you been through in your career?" Members of the audience laughed, and some of them answered three or four. Educators know that a one- or two-year program will probably not produce measurable results before the next superintendent throws it out and introduces his or her own "innovative" curriculum program.

Professional development, particularly for elementary teachers, also shifted away from training in original curriculum design to intensive training in how to follow a prepublished program. But Moody and Stricker (2009) believe that we must shift our energies "toward what is most important—training teachers to utilize their individual knowledge, experience, and creativity to strategically design standards-based classroom instruction" (p. 19). Teachers know their students' interests and abilities better than a textbook company targeting hundreds or thousands of districts. They should be able to design original, differentiated learning experiences that address curriculum goals and state standards.

How Can the Curriculum Spark Student Interest?

When teams of teachers work together to develop meaningful and creative lessons and units, they not only target the standards, but they also engage their learners to take responsibility for their own learning. Pogrow (2009) advocates a technique called Outrageous Instruction. He suggests that teachers use

> a dramatic . . . storyline to create an imaginary context in which the need for the content objective is critical to solving a problem that is of interest to students. When the storyline taps into students' sense of imagination and self, it is then "Creatively Authentic." The creatively authentic lesson or unit then becomes the primary method for teaching that content objective. (p. 379)

Pogrow gives an example of one teacher who dressed up in overalls, wore a white beard and Amish-style black hat, and carried a tree stump. The "master salesman" tried to use his powers of verbal persuasion to convince students to buy his tree stump. He built a sales presentation giving dozens of reasons to buy it.

Later, the master salesman divided the class into groups and asked each one to choose an item from an assortment of common objects and prepare a sales presentation to sell it to the class. Students in each group prepared and delivered a creative sales presentation to persuade their classmates to buy their item. At the end, the teacher explained that each group had just prepared an "oral" persuasive essay similar to the type of written essay required for promotion to the next grade and that the skills they demonstrated in their oral presentation could be transferred to a written essay. In referring to this use of Outrageous Instruction, Pogrow states, "This lesson demonstrates the latent talent, ability, and creativity that reside within our most academically resistant students. . . . However, it also raises the question of why we don't make a greater effort to create such alternative, dramatic approaches" (2009, p. 381). When teachers take risks and use more dramatic and imaginative approaches to teaching the curriculum, students are more willing to become creative themselves. Teaching may revolve around the standards, but it is the curriculum that makes the standards come alive.

In addition to Pogrow's Outrageous Instruction technique, Graseck (2009) advocates that educators do more to awaken student voice by "teaching with controversy." She believes that teachers who address controversial topics like immigration, health-care reform, the environment, war, and the economy challenge students to become competent and responsible citizens who will be able to participate thoughtfully in public debates on issues affecting their lives. Graseck argues that "high school is the last universal stop on the path to adulthood and full citizenship. Here, students can and should learn to wrestle collectively with important public issues they will encounter as 21st-century citizens, including controversial issues" (2009, p. 46). Students conduct research, present oral and written arguments, debate issues, conduct interviews, and write position papers and letters to politicians supporting their viewpoints. They learn the skills of problem solving, decision making, exploring multiple perspectives, analyzing data, examining sources, and making judgments based on evidence. Probably most importantly, students who engage in a controversial discussion embedded in an authentic task learn that there is no one right answer to their problem. Graseck says that "students should be actively analyzing multiple perspectives in light of solid information and learning to wrestle respectfully with competing values to come to their own considered judgment on the issue" (2009, p. 48). Since controversial issues play such a big role in students' lives, teachers should prepare students to address them skillfully.

What Are Performance Tasks?

The two approaches described in the preceding section (Outrageous Instruction and teaching with controversy) both use *performance tasks* to make the curriculum more interesting. Nitko (2004, p. 238) defines a performance task as "an assessment activity that requires a student to demonstrate her achievement by producing an extended written or spoken answer, by engaging in group or individual activities, or by creating a specific product." Performance tasks can be used to assess the *product* the student creates to prove he or she has met the standards as well as the *process* the student uses to complete the product or performance. Students demonstrate their knowledge, skills, and problem-solving abilities as they apply what they have learned in the context of an authentic task.

The required performance can be short and focused on only one or two standards, or it can be extensive and focused on multiple standards. A single-focused performance task might require students to measure the dimensions of a classroom, write a letter to the editor, debate a controversial topic, compare and contrast two national leaders, or write a sonnet about love. A multifocused or extended performance task might require students to create a schoolwide campaign to raise awareness about healthy eating habits in order to reduce childhood obesity. This task could last for several weeks and involve students working in groups to create school lunch menus, design posters, organize school assemblies, and write articles for the school newspaper. Multiple standards related to research, technology, reading, writing, mathematics, science, and oral presentations could be addressed throughout this performance task unit.

Designing Performance Tasks

Performance tasks are best designed by teams of teachers. When the teams develop the tasks, they should always consider the following factors:

- Relationship to standards—Tasks should target the power standards as well as any additional standards that relate to the completion of the tasks. For example, a student writing an editorial about global warming would use the content from a science standard but would also address the process standards related to research, reading, writing, and technology. The task requirements would include the language of the standard to ensure students' understanding of key concepts.

- Relevancy—Tasks should simulate real-life topics or problems that tie into the students' lives. Authentic tasks correlated to standards and meaningful learning experiences motivate students and make learning more memorable now and more transferable to life in the twenty-first century.

- Structure—Some tasks are highly structured or prescriptive so that students know exactly what they are supposed to do. Other tasks are open ended or ill structured to challenge students to engage in higher-order thinking, critical problem solving, and creative expression.

- Grouping—Tasks can accommodate different groupings that are based on students' readiness, interests, or preferred modes of learning. The products or projects that the groups complete vary, depending on students' choices of presentation methods. Students working in teams learn how to use appropriate social skills for interactions and learn how to understand and appreciate one another's differences. Group discussions on content issues can have a profound influence on students' cognitive development (Vygotsky, 1978).

- Rigor—Tasks should reflect high expectations for all students, regardless of their readiness levels. Some students may need different strategies or a different time allotment, but all students should be provided with what Tomlinson (as cited in Rebora, 2008) calls "respectful tasks" so that everybody's work is equally motivating, equally relevant, and equally important.

- Subjectivity—Most performance tasks cannot be assessed by objective-style tests. Because of the performance components, tasks are subjective and need to be assessed using criterion-based tools such as checklists or rubrics. Checklists and rubrics provide scaffolding to support students' understanding of the standards, but they also allow for individuality, creativity, originality, and independence.

- Cognitive level—Tasks require students to go beyond the recall and comprehension levels of Bloom's Taxonomy and utilize the higher levels of application, synthesis, evaluation, and creation of original ideas. Students must make decisions and use appropriate critical and creative problem-solving skills to demonstrate deep understanding of key concepts and the ability to transfer that understanding to other areas of life, including the workplace.

Figure 4.1 (page 54) provides a performance task template for teacher teams to use to create a short, single-focused performance task that can be completed in one or two class periods. The template asks for the following information: performance task title; grade level, subject area, and date; standard; grade-level expectations; curriculum unit; performance task scenario; group work; individual work; differentiation strategies; and assessment. The template can be modified to address only individual work, only group work, or a combination of both individual and group work, depending on the standard and the structure of the task.

Performance task title:

Grade level: Class/subject area: Date:

Standard:

Grade-level expectations:

Curriculum unit:

Performance task scenario (hook to motivate the students):

Group work:

Individual work:

Differentiation:

　How can you adjust the content, process, or product to *support* struggling students?

　How can you adjust the content, process, or product to *challenge* students to extend their thinking?

Assessment:

Adapted from template created by Eileen Depka, Elmbrook Schools, Brookfield, Wisconsin.

Figure 4.1: Performance task template.

In figure 4.2, the template has been used to describe a single-focused math performance task for a third-grade unit on measurement. Teachers could add a group-work component to this task by dividing students into differentiated groups, according to their interests or abilities, and asking the groups to complete the assignment.

Desk Dilemma: Choosing Measurement Tools

Grade level: 3   **Class/subject area:** Math   **Date:**

Standard: Students will measure length using appropriate units and tools.

Grade-level expectations: Students choose from appropriate tools such as ruler, yardstick, meter stick, or tape measure and start with a "0" on tool to record measurement.

Curriculum unit: Measurement

Performance task scenario (hook to motivate the students): Attention, class! We have a visitor today who has heard about your awesome abilities to measure things correctly using various measurement tools. Miss Smith is a student teacher who will be working in our school next month. Please measure the following items in our class: math book, book shelf, sink, pencil, window pane, window, doorway, smart board, rug, bulletin board, and counter. You may select the tool (ruler, yardstick, meter stick, or tape measure) that provides the most appropriate method to measure the objects. *Let's get started.* Miss Smith wants to observe our skills so she knows what to teach the other third-grade class when she comes to our school next month. We know that when it comes to measurement, *our class rules!*

Individual work: Students are assigned objects at home to measure and bring back the information to share.

Differentiation:

How can you adjust the content, process, or product to *support* struggling students?

1   Let students work with a partner.

2   Have students check in with the teacher more often to make sure they understand the assignment.

3   Assign students fewer items to measure.

How can you adjust the content, process, or product to *challenge* students to extend their thinking?

1   Assign students more difficult items to measure.

2   Ask students to measure the same item in two different systems.

3   Ask students to compile another list of items from throughout the school.

Assessment: Use grid that includes:

Item Measured	Measurement Tool	Length of Item	Width of Item

Created by Kate Arnold, Daphne Hall, Lisa Lane, and Lisa Stanzi; Clarke County School District; Athens, Georgia. Used with permission.

Figure 4.2: Grade-3 mathematics performance task.

Figure 4.3 gives the specifications for a science performance task. This task requires students to work in small groups to pose and answer questions about the different states of water integral to precipitation, condensation, and evaporation.

H₂O: Where Did You Go? Weather Unit

Grade level: 4   **Class/subject area:** Science   **Date:**

Standard: Students will explain the water cycle (evaporation, condensation, precipitation).

Grade-level expectations: How are different states of water integral to precipitation, condensation, and evaporation?

Curriculum unit: Water cycle

Performance task scenario (hook to motivate the students): The local Science Center needs a display to explain the water cycle to visitors. Because of your vast expertise in science, the director of the Science Center would like our class to create a poster on which we draw and label a diagram of the water cycle and define the words *evaporation*, *condensation*, and *precipitation*. She would also like us to design three stations where we pose a scientific question and then provide the answer.

Station 1:

Question: It rained this morning, and then the sun came out. Now the ground is dry. Where did the water go?

Answer:

Station 2:

Question: Mom put a glass of lemonade on the table. When I sat down to dinner, there was water on the outside of the glass. Where did the water come from?

Answer:

Station 3:

Question: There are clouds covering the sun. What might happen soon, and why?

Answer:

Differentiation:

   How can you adjust the content, process, or product to *support* struggling students?

  1   Pictures of examples of precipitation, condensation, and evaporation will be provided for some students.

Figure 4.3: Grade-4 science performance task.

2   Word cards will be provided for students to match words to pictures.

How can you adjust the content, process, or product to *challenge* students to extend their thinking?

1   Students will create a PowerPoint presentation to illustrate the water cycle.

Assessment: Teacher will observe students and ask them to explain the rationale for their answers to the questions.

Created by Carrie Bette-Duncan, Scherry Lewis, Barbara Michalove, Halley Page, and Claire Smith; Clarke County School District; Athens, Georgia. Used with permission.

Group Performance Tasks

Some performance tasks focus on group activities that require students to apply their knowledge and skills in a collaborative effort. Group performance tasks encourage students to explore and honor multiple viewpoints. Students who see the importance of understanding, respecting, and responding to other people's points of view develop what Sternberg (1985, 1988) calls "practical intelligence." This ability to get along with others or to see things and oneself as others do is different from the ability to do well on tests in school. Understanding another person's viewpoint allows students to adapt more easily to the demands of school and life. Sternberg and Williams (1996, p. 41) assert that "few things impede intellectual development and creative performance more than defensiveness against other viewpoints or criticism. Some people don't want to hear anyone else's opinion and if they do, they immediately assume it is wrong—or tune it out." By using cooperative groups as part of a performance task, teachers foster an appreciation of diversity and a respect for other students. Hopefully, that acceptance and tolerance transfer from the classroom, to the school, to the neighborhood, and finally to the world.

Students' perspectives can be further broadened when the collaborative task requires them to imagine themselves in other people's shoes. The middle school performance task "Africa: Unveiling Her Face to the World" asks students both to cooperate with others and to see the world from a different point of view. As shown in figure 4.4 (page 58), this assignment presents a powerful and authentic hook that allows students to showcase their creativity as well as their knowledge of the standards. Students choose one of four projects that focus on the conditions of children in Africa: creating a photo essay, a talk show, an educational board game, or a greeting card.

Some students like the visual challenge of creating a photo essay or greeting card, others enjoy the logical and creative aspects of designing a board game, and others enjoy the interpersonal and verbal experiences of presenting a talk show. Giving students options for expressing their creativity and displaying their understanding of the standards is motivating and inspires engaged learning. Vatterott (2009) believes that tasks promote ownership when they allow for choices, offer students a chance to personalize their work, and tap students' emotions, feelings, or opinions about a subject.

Africa: Unveiling Her Face to the World Social Studies Unit

Middle school social studies standard: The student will describe major developments in Africa since independence. Describe problems created by health issues, such as AIDS, and starvation. Explain the problems created by repeated civil war in Africa; include the Democratic Republic of the Congo and Rwanda.

Problem scenario:

Dear Oprah,

My name is Nzuri. This is Swahili for "beauty." Recently I heard about the school that you opened for young girls in South Africa. I dream of one day being able to attend school, but in my country, we are not as fortunate. I am a 12-year-old girl from a village in the Darfur region of Africa where people have been affected by ethnic and political conflict for years. Like many children in my village, I do not have enough food, clean water, medicine, or protection, and I have never been to a real school like the one you opened. Our school is a broken-down box cart that is three miles away from my home. I know that if you came to my country, you would be able to help the children in my village. And one day my dream would come true. I would become a teacher and be able to help the people in my village. Oprah, can you help give the children of my country what they need to survive?

Your friend,

Nzuri

Dear Nzuri,

In response to your letter, Oprah has decided to come to your village. Your task is to unveil the face of your village so that the world sees the "beauty" in the faces of the children and responds to your need for help. So that we can showcase your village to the world, the children of your village must prepare one of the following projects:

1   Create a photo essay that shows the faces of one of the following—AIDS, Education, War, Hunger, or Poverty.

2   Create a talk show with children from various ethnic backgrounds sharing information about their cultures.

3   Create an educational board game describing the beauty of your village.

4   Design greeting cards to focus on various social, political, or cultural issues within this region.

Oprah's advance team will visit your village on _____ to review your projects in preparation for Oprah's visit and the filming of a special documentary later in the month.

Director of Documentaries
Harpo Productions
Chicago, IL

Created by Yvonne Stroud, DeKalb County School System, Decatur, Georgia. Used with permission.

Figure 4.4: Middle school collaborative performance task.

How Can Performance Tasks Be Assessed?

By creating user-friendly assessment tools, teachers help their students self-assess both individual and group work in performance tasks. Checklists and rubrics provide valuable tools to help students work through a standards-based *process* as they complete the final *product* in the performance task. Figure 4.5 is a checklist for a seventh-grade math performance task. Students have been asked to write a letter to their friend Bobo, who unfortunately fell out of a tree and missed an important lesson on positive and negative rational numbers (integers). The students' letters are to describe the four operations and give examples of each. The checklist "chunks" the different steps and operations involved in the performance task and provides columns for students to check off "Not Yet" if they have not completed the step or "Yes" if they have.

To differentiate this assignment to help students who are struggling to understand the mathematical concepts, teachers can allow some students to work in pairs. Struggling students may need another partner to help them with their writing skills when they proofread their letters. To differentiate this assignment to challenge students who finish it quickly, teachers might ask them to record a three-minute video explaining the process to Bobo and asking for any questions he might have. These students could also create five math problems involving integers to send to Bobo and then correct the answers and clarify any misunderstandings he might have through email messages or phone conversations. To add to the overall authenticity of the task, one of the students could role-play Bobo. Or there might be a student who was really absent and needs the tutoring, even if he did not fall out of a tree and break both legs!

Letter to Bobo Explaining Integers: Honors Math 7

Standard: M7N1: Students will understand the meaning of positive and negative rational numbers and use them in computation.

Task: Your classmate, Bobo, fell out of a tree! He broke both of his legs and is confined to bed for a while. He has missed our unit on positive and negative rational numbers (integers). As a good friend, you are going to write Bobo a letter explaining how to compute positive and negative rational numbers. Include all rules for the four operations and give three examples of each. You need to have the letter to me by _____, so that Bobo will get the letter in time to study for the chapter test.

Assignment: Self-assess your letter to Bobo by reviewing the criteria and giving yourself a rating of "Not Yet" or "Yes" in the right-hand column.	Not Yet 0	Yes 1
Letter format: Did you include . . .		
Date (for example, January 10, 2010)?		

Figure 4.5: Checklist for "Letter to Bobo" performance task.

continued on next page →

	Not Yet 0	Yes 1
Salutation (greeting) (for example, Dear Bobo,)?		
Body—6 paragraphs?		
Closing (for example, Sincerely,)?		
Signature (your name)?		
Paragraph 1—Introduction: Did you have . . .		
Sentiment (I am sorry . . .)?		
Topic sentence (I am writing to . . .)?		
Transition (Now I am going to tell you . . .)?		
At least three sentences?		
Paragraph 2—Adding integers: Did you provide . . .		
The rule for adding with like signs?		
Three examples with like signs?		
The rule for adding with unlike signs?		
Three examples with unlike signs?		
Paragraph 3—Subtracting integers: Did you provide . . .		
The rule for subtracting integers?		
Three examples for subtracting?		
Paragraph 4—Multiplying integers: Did you provide . . .		
The rule for multiplying with like signs?		
Three examples with like signs?		

	Not Yet 0	Yes 1
The rule for multiplying with unlike signs?		
Three examples with unlike signs?		
Paragraph 5—Dividing integers: Did you provide . . .		
The rule for dividing with like signs?		
Three examples with like signs?		
The rule for dividing with unlike signs?		
Three examples with unlike signs?		
Paragraph 6—Conclusion: Did you . . .		
Use a transition (word or phrase)?		
Repeat topic sentence (why you are writing)?		
Conclude with friendly personal sentence (for example, I'll see you when you get back.)?		
Write at least three sentences?		
Final product: Is your letter . . .		
Typed and double spaced?		
At least 2 pages in length?		
Free of spelling and grammar errors?		

continued on next page →

Add up your points to determine the grade you would receive if this were your final product.

Total points: _____/30

Grading scale
A = 27–30
B = 24–26
C = 21–23
F = 0–20

Final grade _____

What do you need to do to improve this letter before it is graded by the teacher next week?

Student signature _____

Created by Patti Allen and Matilda Strickland; Carrollton Junior High School; Carrollton City Schools; Carrollton, Georgia. Used with permission.

What Are Some Other Examples of Performance Tasks?

Math teachers have been using performance tasks for years. Story problems require students to apply their math skills in order to solve a real-life problem. Figure 4.6 shows a fourth-grade group performance task for a unit on graphing. The task addresses one math standard by challenging students to solve the infamous "snack thief dilemma." Note that the teachers who designed this task modified the template to include content for whole-class instruction, vocabulary, and assignments and assessments for individual work.

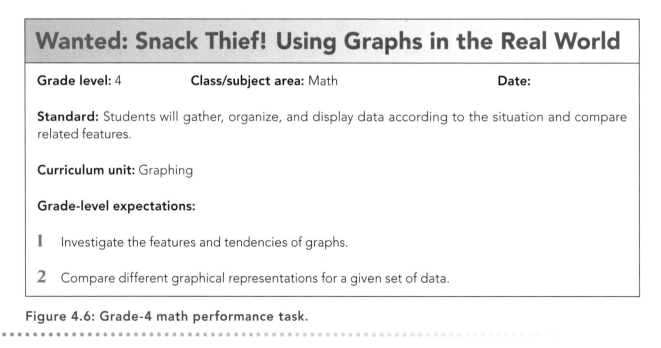

Wanted: Snack Thief! Using Graphs in the Real World

Grade level: 4   **Class/subject area:** Math   **Date:**

Standard: Students will gather, organize, and display data according to the situation and compare related features.

Curriculum unit: Graphing

Grade-level expectations:

1   Investigate the features and tendencies of graphs.

2   Compare different graphical representations for a given set of data.

Figure 4.6: Grade-4 math performance task.

Performance task scenario (hook to motivate the students): Attention, all students! There is snack thief loose in our school. YIKES! Snacks are disappearing from the cafeteria. What will we do? We need to know which snack is being swiped the most so we can set a trap! Ta-da! The thief is taking bites from several snack bags. Please help us save our snacks, or we'll have to eat brussel sprouts for our snack tomorrow! YUCK! Each team needs to figure out which snack the thief is stealing the most.

Here's how you and your team can help!

1   Count the items in each snack bag: carrots, raisins, pretzels, and teddy grahams.

2   Create a graph comparing the number of snack items in each bag.

3   Determine the range of snack data that your team collected.

4   Determine whether or not the snack thief has been pilfering your particular snack or not.

Group 1—*Carrots*   Group 2—*Raisins*   Group 3—*Pretzels*   Group 4— *Teddy grahams*

  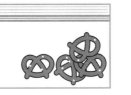 

Whole-class instruction: List the content or skills that will be introduced to prepare students for the group and individual work.

● How to gather data

● How to create graphs from data collected

● How to interpret data

● How to calculate range

● How to report data

● How to draw conclusions from collected data

Vocabulary

Data, bar graph, pictograph, range

Individual work: Each student will complete the following:

1   Create a graph (pictograph or bar graph) using the range of each snack to determine which snack is being snitched.

continued on next page →

2   Create a final project stating the evidence you used to solve this *tummy grumbling crime* (poster, oral news report, detailed crime report, or other reporting option approved by the chief of police).

Methods of Assessment:

● Checklist for group work

● Checklist for graphs

● Observation

● Rubric for police report

Created by Molly Efland, Laura Forehand, Brian Madej, Joyce Moeller, and Jenna Starnes; Clarke County School District; Athens, Georgia. Used with permission.

Teachers are sometimes reluctant to assign group work in class because students tend to misbehave or get off-task easily, especially if they are confused about what they are supposed to do. It is helpful for teachers to create a group checklist that shows students the steps they need to take to complete their assigned task. Figure 4.7 is the group checklist for the "Snack Thief" performance task. It guides students through the steps of gathering, representing, interpreting, and reporting data and helps them self-assess their progress.

Group Checklist for "Wanted: Snack Thief!"

Math standard: Students will gather, organize, and display data according to the situation and compare related features.

Assignment: Use this checklist to guide you as you complete your task and to self-assess your work.

	Not Yet 0	Yes 1
Gathering data		
Did you count and check the items in each snack bag?		
What is the amount in each snack bag? Bag 1 (Carrots) _____ Bag 2 (Raisins) _____ Bag 3 (Pretzels) _____ Bag 4 (Teddy grahams) _____		
Representing data		
Did you make a graph of the data you collected?		

Figure 4.7: Group-work checklist for grade-4 math performance task.

	Not Yet 0	Yes 1
What kind of graph did you use? _____		
Interpreting data		
Did you determine the range of the snack data?		
What is the range? _____		
Using the range, do you think the snack thief has been stealing your snack? _____		
List your evidence: _____ _____ _____		
Reporting data		
Did you use your checklist to report your data to the class?		
Social skills		
Did you speak politely to each other?		
Did you all stay on task?		
Did you each contribute to the group?		
Did you all listen politely to each other?		

Created by Molly Efland, Laura Forehand, Brian Madej, Joyce Moeller, and Jenna Starnes; Clarke County School District; Athens, Georgia. Used with permission.

The checklist ensures that students in each group understand what they are expected to know and do. As they go through the steps, the teacher monitors the process, clarifying difficult concepts when students are struggling. By providing ongoing specific feedback throughout the process, teachers prevent minor confusion from escalating into major misunderstandings that could impact subsequent math instruction.

When students work on group performance tasks, it is a good idea to assign each student an individual task at the end of the unit to check for understanding. In this way, the teacher certifies that each student—not just a few group members—really understands the key concept. Figure 4.8 (page 66) is a science performance task that helps students understand the concept by working in groups with their peers. This same task then uses individual work to provide evidence that each student does, in fact, understand the concept and can apply it appropriately.

Changes in the "Nye"ght: Science Unit

Grade level: 5   **Class/subject area:** Science   **Date:**

Standard: Students will understand the differences between physical and chemical changes.

Curriculum unit: Physical and Chemical Change

Performance task scenario (hook to motivate the students): We have a science emergency! As you know, Bill Nye, "the Science Guy," was going to come to our school's *Family Science Night* next Friday. We just received a fax that Bill Nye has fizzled out with the fall flu. Our principal, Mr. Guy, has asked our fabulous fifth-grade class members to fill in for Nye and set up science stations for our families. For the Science Night we will need to: 1) demonstrate physical change by manipulating paper; 2) demonstrate physical change by separating mixtures (oil/water); 3) collect data on the temperature of water in various states (water vapor/steam, liquid, ice); 4) investigate the properties of a match before, during, and after being lit (chemical reaction); 5) investigate the properties of oobleck ingredients before, during, and after making it. *Let's get started.* You need to construct your assigned science station by next Thursday so we can have a rehearsal before the parents come on Friday night.

Group work: Students may select their topic or presentation method.

Station 1	Station 2	Station 3	Station 4	Station 5
Create a poster that illustrates how manipulating paper is a physical change. Show examples of cutting, tearing, and folding.	Demonstrate physical change by separating mixtures. Set up 2 live demos; explain why what is observed is an example of physical change.	Create a bar graph showing the temperature of water in various states. Use the data from your science journal.	Light a match and take pictures of the before, during, and after. Prepare a PowerPoint presentation that explains the chemical change that occurred.	Make oobleck and take pictures of the before, during, and after. Prepare a PowerPoint presentation that explains the chemical change that occurred.

Individual work: Each student will complete the following:

1   Collect and record data in your science journal on chemical changes.

2   Collect and record data in your science journal on physical changes.

3   Write an essay comparing chemical and physical changes by analyzing the data you collected.

Figure 4.8: Grade-5 science performance task.

Differentiation:

How can you adjust the content, process, or product to *support* struggling students?

Provide a checklist for the student journal.

How can you adjust the content, process, or product to *challenge* students to extend their thinking?

Require students to demonstrate creativity in order to receive a "4" in their Science Journal Rubric.

Assessment: Rubric for Science Journal

Created by Jan Miller-Burkins, Karen Higginbotham, Bertha Troutman-Rambeau, and Hallie Williamson; Clarke County School District; Athens, Georgia. Used with permission.

One way to differentiate the individual journal assignment is to provide a checklist to help students who may have problems writing about physical and chemical change in their student journals. Figure 4.9 shows how the teacher chunked the process by dividing it into "Organization of Journal" and "Experiment Content."

Student Journal Individual Checklist

S5P2: Physical and Chemical Change

Standard: Students will understand the differences between physical and chemical changes.

Assignment: Students will collect and record data on both chemical and physical change in a science journal and self-assess their work using this checklist.

	Not Yet 0	Yes 1
Organization of journal		
Did you include a cover sheet with a title?		
Did you include a cover sheet with your name?		
Did you put a date on all entries?		
Did your table of contents include a title?		

Figure 4.9: Individual checklist for grade-5 science journal.

continued on next page →

	Not Yet 0	Yes 1
Did your table of contents include the titles and page numbers of all experiments?		
Did you have a page number on each page?		
Experiment content		
In *each* experiment did you include your . . .		
Title? List one _____		
Date?		
Hypothesis? (What do you think will happen?) List one _____		
Materials list?		
Experimental procedures? (Experiment instructions)		
Observation notes? (Did you record your notes?) One observation was _____ _____		
Analysis of the results? (Includes notes and illustrations or graphs) How many graphs did you include? _____		
Conclusion? What is it? _____		

Created by Jan Miller-Burkins, Karen Higginbotham, Bertha Troutman-Rambeau, and Hallie Williamson; Clarke County School District; Athens, Georgia. Used with permission.

The final example of a performance task (fig. 4.10) was written for high school Latin students. The class is divided into groups to design an art museum for ancient Rome. Each group selects a topic ranging from sculptures to jewelry, creates an exhibit brochure, and contributes to a class-created wiki page that will serve as a virtual museum. It is important to note that students may choose the topic that most interests them, as well as the format and layout of their brochure. They are required, however, to include specific elements related to the standard, such as a picture of each art piece, a brief description of the piece in English, and information about whether the piece was primarily decorative or functional. The task thus combines teacher guidelines to target curriculum goals and student choice to encourage creativity and problem solving.

An Art Museum for Ancient Rome: Latin Unit

Grade level: High school   **Class/subject area:** Latin 3   **Date:**

Standard: Students will understand the culture of Ancient Rome.

Curriculum unit: Culture

Performance task scenario (hook to motivate the students): The year is 25 BC, and the new Emperor Augustus has commissioned you, his closest advisors, to help design a new national art museum to rival the fame of Alexandria's library and renew Roman patriotism. Unfortunately, decades of civil war have drained imperial funds, and space will be limited. As experts on a particular medium of Roman artwork, it is your task to select and prepare four to five pieces of artwork that you feel best represent Roman history, values, and practices. Remember to do your best work, because you don't want to become the *main feature* at the next sporting event at the Coliseum!

Group work: Students may select their topic and some aspects of their presentation method.

Group topics

Sculpture: Marble statues, bronze statues, reliefs, sarcophagi

Mosaics: All tiled surfaces

Pottery and glass: Everyday pottery, decorative vases, plates, glass bowls

Paintings: Paintings on wood, fresco wall murals

Jewelry and mirrors: Handheld mirrors (Etruscan), various jewelry, belts, armor

Exhibit brochure: Each group must create a simple but informative brochure for visitors to their section of the museum. The group may choose the format and layout of the brochure, but it must include a picture of each piece of artwork in the exhibit, accompanied by a brief description of it in English. The brochure should also address, in English, how the Romans made and used this type of artwork and whether the primary purpose was decorative or functional in nature.

Virtual museum: Each group must contribute to the class-created wiki page, which will serve as a virtual museum of the selected art pieces. Students should upload pictures of their artwork with English descriptions and medium information on a separate page. All groups should also contribute ideas to the museum's homepage, which should entice Roman citizens to come and visit.

Figure 4.10: High school Latin performance task.

continued on next page →

Differentiation:

How can you adjust the content, process, or product to *support* struggling students?

| Provide a checklist for the brochure and virtual museum.

How can you adjust the content, process, or product to *challenge* students to extend their thinking?

| Students can translate the brochure and provide a copy in Latin as well as English.

Assessment: Checklist for exhibit brochure and virtual museum

---

Created by Whitney Slough for the Foreign Language Instructional Planning course taught by Janet D. Parker, College of William and Mary, spring 2009. Used with permission.

The checklist that corresponds to this task (fig. 4.11) provides the scaffolding for completing the group brochure and virtual museum page. Even advanced or gifted students need some scaffolding if they are attempting an assignment they have never done before. The teacher may decide to assign the next project without providing a checklist for guidance because he or she wants to know if the students have internalized the criteria and can work independently to demonstrate their mastery of the concepts and the process.

Group Brochure and Virtual Museum Page Student Checklist

Self-assess your brochure and virtual museum page using this checklist.	Not Yet 0	Yes 1
Collaborative process		
Are you doing your share?		
Does everyone in your group have one art piece on which to concentrate?		
Exhibit brochure		
Have you used multiple, reliable sources in your research?		
Would your brochure inspire patriotism in a fellow Roman?		

Figure 4.11: Student checklist for high school Latin performance task.

	Not Yet 0	Yes 1
Is the brochure neatly organized?		
Is the brochure eye-catching?		
Do you have a picture of an art piece from every group member?		
Do you have an English description from every group member?		
Do all the English descriptions mention the following: medium, year made, artist (if known), and significance?		
Does the brochure describe how this type of art form was used?		
Does the brochure describe how this type of art was made?		
Have you double-checked for typos and grammatical errors?		
Virtual museum		
Do you have a picture from each group member?		
Do you have an English description from every group member (same as in the brochure)?		
Have you double-checked for typos and grammatical errors?		
Have you included information about how this art was made and used?		
Are ALL of your group members contributing actively to creating an eye-catching homepage?		
Does your exhibit page stand out and make the viewer want to learn more?		

Created by Whitney Slough for the Foreign Language Instructional Planning course taught by Janet D. Parker, College of William and Mary, spring 2009. Used with permission.

Final Thoughts

Just as many students continually ask their teachers, "Why do we have to do this?" some teachers ask their district leaders, "Why do we have to do *this*?" The "this" refers to changing their curriculum to reflect the challenges and goals of life in the twenty-first century. Many students feel they leave their twenty-first-century world behind when they enter their school. Copying definitions, memorizing dates, filling out worksheets, writing on chalkboards, and taking paper-and-pencil tests are more appropriate for the factory-model schools of the nineteenth century than for the schools of the twenty-first century. Erkens (2009, p. 19) argues that since "the rate of information is doubling faster than we can produce new books," assessment should focus on preparing students for the future. Students today need to learn how to deal with controversial social and political problems, technological advances, and global economic challenges.

It is evident that performance tasks provide a motivational framework by introducing real-life scenarios requiring students to demonstrate their understanding and apply their skills. These tasks relate directly to students' lives as either real or hypothetical problems that pique their interest, require their participation, and spark their creative and critical thinking abilities. Darling-Hammond and McCloskey (2008) believe that when teachers use and evaluate these tasks, "they become more knowledgeable about both the standards and how to teach them and about their students' learning needs. Thus, the process improves the quality of teaching and learning" (p. 264). They compare performance assessment to practicing driving in preparation for taking the driving test. Everyone knows the requirements for passing the driving test, so the practice focuses on the goals. "In the same way," they note, "performance assessments set a standard towards which everyone must work. The task and the standards are not secret, so teachers and students know what skills they need to develop and how they will need to be demonstrated" (2008, p. 265).

Of course, teachers cannot provide a performance task for every standard, nor can they integrate multiple subject areas, advanced technology, and the use of interpersonal skills into every lesson. The curriculum, however, must reflect the knowledge and skills that students need to be successful in the twenty-first century. When young people today approach a problem, they need to know how to access accurate information, solve problems, analyze data, communicate effectively, interact socially, make good decisions, and think critically and creatively. By applying these skills in addition to their content knowledge, students simulate solving problems in the world beyond school and will be prepared to tackle life's authentic performance tasks.

Concluding Exercises

Reflections on Performance Tasks

1 Who creates the curriculum in your school, subject area, or district?

2 Why should students be taught how to solve problem scenarios embedded in performance tasks?

3 How could teachers create common performance tasks to use with all the students in a grade or subject-area class?

4 Why should common assessments, such as checklists and rubrics, accompany performance tasks?

Action Steps

List three action steps you plan to take to create more performance task units as part of your curriculum.

Step 1:

Step 2:

Step 3:

5

Checklists: Progressions of Learning

Examples of checklists have appeared throughout the preceding chapters. This chapter will explore in more detail the various types and uses of checklists and will discuss how to create high-quality checklists correlated to curriculum goals and standards.

What Are Checklists?

When most people hear the word *checklist*, they probably think of a "to-do" list for the day, a pilot's preflight checklist, or a first-day-of-school checklist for a beginning teacher. Rarely do people think of checklists as one of a teacher's most valuable instructional *and* assessment tools. Nor do they think of a checklist as a helpful organizational and study skill tool for students. The dual nature of the checklist allows it to provide both instructional guidance and formative feedback on an ongoing basis.

A checklist used in education is also called a *learning progression*. Popham (2008, p. 24) explains that a learning progression "is composed of the step-by-step building blocks students are presumed to need in order to successfully attain a more distant, designated instructional outcome." For example, if the targeted curricular goal is writing a persuasive essay, students will need to master several smaller cognitive subskills, such as researching pertinent information, formulating a thesis statement, organizing the essay, and using appropriate grammar and mechanics.

Checklists make a complex, multistep task more manageable for both teaching and learning. They have the power to prevent students from failing or falling between the cracks. They serve as *scaffolding* to support, guide, and direct students as they work through a task or process. The more scaffolding the teacher provides—for example, the more tactics the teacher suggests to the student—the more structured the task (Nitko, 2004). A task is considered unstructured if there are many equally valid alternative pathways to the correct answer or to the final product. Teachers may provide more scaffolding or structure the first time they assign a task or when they assign a difficult task that requires multiple steps to complete.

The key to success for many students is completing each subskill or chunk that is a smaller component of a larger instructional outcome. For example, the instructional outcome of writing a persuasive essay could be overwhelming to many students. Students may not know where to start, they may forget some of the essential components, and they almost always forget what the teacher told them in class. But they slowly gain confidence when they use a roadmap—a checklist—to guide them through the process. Returning to the grade-7 persuasive essay checklist shown in figure 3.3 (page 37), we see how it breaks the whole essay into manageable subskills or chunks so that students can focus on each step by answering questions and completing the subskill before moving on. The checklist divides the essay into paragraphs and breaks the paragraphs down into parts. For example, the introductory paragraph is broken down into two parts, labeled A and B, and each part has a set of questions to help the student complete the steps. The following segment extracted from the checklist shows how it guides the student through the introductory paragraph.

    A. Does my writing **ENGAGE THE READER?**

        1   Is my **PURPOSE** in writing clear? (to persuade)

        2   Do I create a "**SPEAKER'S VOICE**"?

        3   Do I use one of the following strategies to **DEVELOP READER INTEREST**?

            —Question

            —Startling fact

            —Scenario

            —Dazzling description

            —Anecdote

            —Quotation

    B. Do I state a **CLEAR POSITION** or **PERSPECTIVE** in support of my proposition or proposal?

        1   Is the **PROBLEM** clear to the reader?

        2   Is my **OPINION** clear to the reader?

        3   Do I have a clearly developed **THESIS STATEMENT**?

As noted in chapter 3, the language of the standards (LOTS) appears in boldface capital letters so that teachers know they are targeting the key words and important concepts that the students will encounter on the high-stakes standardized tests. When students see these words and phrases emphasized on the checklist, they in turn become very aware of the important terminology embedded in the standards and will be able to recognize the key terms throughout their school careers.

Checklists or learning progressions are also essential for implementing formative assessment because they provide checkpoints to determine whether students are on track to meet their learning goals. Popham (2008, p. 27) notes that the checklist framework "helps teachers identify appropriate adjustment-decision points as well as the kinds of en route assessment evidence they need." Formative assessment is built around these adjustment-decision points that pave the way to producing quality work.

Based on their assessments, teachers decide if and when they need to add building blocks, change the sequence, stop and reteach certain skills, or extend blocks to challenge learners who have mastered the task quickly and become bored or disruptive while waiting for the struggling students to learn the skills. Although the checklist represents the teacher's best-judgment hypothesis of how the greatest number of students will learn, the effective teacher knows that there will never be a one-size-fits-all sequence. Therefore, teachers must be ready to differentiate their instruction to help all students master the targeted curricular goal (Popham, 2008). The checklist provides a roadmap to the standards, but there will be many detours along the journey.

What Are the Components of a Checklist?

Each checklist may consist of slightly different components, depending on its purpose. Some of the most common components include the following:

1   Title of checklist (name of task being assessed)

2   Student's name, class, period, date

3   Standard or standards being addressed with the checklist

4   A brief description of the task or assignment the students are completing

5   The major categories of the performance indicators for the task. These categories are listed in bold in the shaded rows of the checklist so that students know they represent the big "chunks" of the task. They are organized in sequential order so that students see the logical development of the process or product.

6   Subpoints or subskills, listed under each major category. The subskills should be indented and possibly bulleted. They are usually presented in question format to help students self-assess whether they have completed that part of the task.

7   Scoring columns to the right of the checklist for the purpose of rating the subskills. The ratings may be as simple as "Not Yet" or "Yes" to indicate whether a step has been completed. The scoring columns may also designate a numerical score of a 0 or a 1 so that students can add up their points to find out how they did on the assignment.

8   A section for students to write comments about how they think they did on the assignment and a place for teacher feedback and the signatures of both the student and the teacher

9   A scale that shows how the point values accrued by the student translate into a letter grade, a percentage grade, or a proficiency level

If it is early in the learning period and students have just been introduced to new material or a new project or performance, the numerical scores and scale could be omitted, because the primary purpose of the checklist is to serve as a formative assessment that will provide initial feedback. On the other hand, if students have been working on the assignment and have already received feedback and been given opportunities for revisions, further practice, or do-overs, the purpose of the checklist will be to assign the final summative grade. In that case, the point system and scale are necessary and should reflect the grading policy of the school and district.

Figure 5.1 (page 78) provides a template that teachers can use to develop student checklists for a group or an individual task. The "Not Yet" and "Yes" ratings can be changed to reflect the feedback each teacher wants to use (for example, "Do Over" and "In Progress"). Also, the scores of 0 and 1 can be eliminated if teachers do not want students to be concerned about points or grades during the beginning "practice," "novice," or "do-over" stages of a project or performance.

Title of checklist: _____		
Student: _____ Class: _____		
Period: _____ Date: _____		
Standard: _____		
Assignment: _____		

Performance Indicators	Not Yet 0	Yes 1
Main Category: _____		
●		
●		
●		
Main Category: _____		
●		
●		
●		
Main Category: _____		
●		
●		
●		
Main Category: _____		
●		
●		
●		

Figure 5.1: Template for a student checklist.

Scale	Total Points: _____

Student Comment:

Teacher Comment:

Student Signature: _____

Teacher Signature: _____

The main categories or chunks are the broader, more abstract performance indicators from the standard. They usually appear in shaded rows and are not rated or scored. The items under each main category are the subskills, and they are bulleted and indented so that students have a visual reminder that these are components of the main categories. An example of a main category for writing an essay is "organization." This concept is so broad that students don't really know the expectations. The bullet points under organization are the more concrete subskills, such as "introduction," "support sentences," and "concluding sentence."

How Should Checklists Be Constructed?

As discussed in chapter 3, teams of teachers work together to create common checklists for the individual and group work that students need to master. Figure 5.2 (page 80) provides guidelines to help teachers create student checklists for multistep projects or performances. The guidelines are presented in a checklist format, which breaks the process down into steps, including using the vocabulary from the state standards, chunking the main ideas or categories into three or four steps, arranging the checklist in a sequential or logical order, formatting the checklist so that it is age appropriate, and deciding on rating and scoring options to provide feedback to students (Burke, 2006).

How Are Checklists Used for Assessment and Feedback?

To know if students are benefiting from instruction, teachers must routinely collect and analyze evidence of their performance. Checklists provide a valuable tool for monitoring student progress. As explained in earlier chapters, a checklist can be used as a *diagnostic* tool at the beginning of a task to assess students' readiness levels so that teachers know what they will need to differentiate their instruction. The same checklist could be used as a *formative* assessment throughout the task to help teachers adjust their teaching—to introduce additional instructional strategies to help struggling students succeed and to challenge students who have already mastered the skills. If the purpose of the checklist is to assess the final product after repeated practice rounds, the checklist then becomes a *summative* assessment that *proves* learning and yields a numerical or letter grade.

Teacher Guidelines for Creating Student Checklists

	Not Yet	Yes
Teacher task: Use these guidelines to create a checklist to lead your students through a specific project or performance. Then use this checklist to self-assess your checklist.		
Language of the standards: Did you include . . .		
● The vocabulary from your state standards?		
● Important people and places?		
● Key concepts from the standards?		
"Chunking" the main ideas or categories: Did you . . .		
● Categorize (chunk) parts of the standards that fit together?		
● Limit each chunk to three to five subskills?		
● Rearrange performance indicators under each category so they fit logically?		
Sequential order: Did you . . .		
● Arrange the checklist in the order students would complete the work?		
● Arrange the order so it is developmentally appropriate?		
● Add steps that are necessary for understanding?		

Figure 5.2: Teacher guidelines for creating student checklists.

	Not Yet	Yes
Scoring: Did you . . .		
● Avoid providing scoring columns for the big abstract categories that appear in the shaded rows?		
● Designate one point for a "Yes" or "In Progress" rating?		
● Designate a zero for a "Not Yet" or "Do Over" rating?		
● Provide a scale to give specific feedback to students?		

It is too late to help a student when the final persuasive essay is turned in, because the summative assessment is the last judgment. It makes more sense to monitor each step or chunk of the process and intervene as needed to make sure the student understands the skill before moving on. Many of the skills assessed in checklists are building blocks leading to other standards, and it is easier to repair the foundation of the house *before* the house is built. When checklists are used as formative assessments, they help teachers zero in on a target subskill and figure out the most appropriate intervention to address a problem before students become confused, fall behind, and lose interest.

Using Checklists for Self-Assessment

Checklists make it possible for students to self-assess their own work by looking closely at each step in the sequence and determining whether they have completed it. Students may also use the checklists with a partner or in a cooperative group to assess their peers' work. In these ways, they become more involved with their own learning and assume more accountability for their progress. By including questions in student checklists, teachers can quickly determine if students are on the right track. The questions serve as a cognitive "speed bump" to slow students down and make them reflect on the answers rather than just racing through to see who can check off the steps the fastest.

The formative checklist is sometimes called the "do-over" checklist because as students go through the process of rating themselves, they learn immediately what they have not done, cannot do, or are doing incorrectly, and then they can "do it over." Since formative checklists help *improve* learning, they are considered practice and are not usually graded (although they might affect grades for participation or effort). As explained earlier, some checklists allow students to calculate points for the steps they have completed. The total number of points can be converted into a tentative grade, which shows students how well they are doing in this practice assignment and lets them know what more they have to do before they get a final grade. The process is similar to taking practice college-entrance exams. The practice exams may not count, but students need to know the scores they have received so that they know how they are doing. Data are important for students as well as teachers and administrators.

Using Checklists for Feedback

Many teachers give only oral instructions for assignments and then spend considerable time trying to answer individual students' questions. If teachers give their students written checklists, they do not have to spend as much time answering questions or clarifying their oral instructions. The standardized written guidelines they provide to all the students in the class target the language of the standards, the big ideas, the essential questions, and the curriculum goals for all students. When students have all the oral instructions written on the checklists, they can follow directions at their own pace and self-assess their own work.

The checklists provide feedback as the students go through each step and answer, "Yes, I have done this" or "No, I have not done this." Peers and the teacher can also provide feedback by reviewing a student's work and rating his or her progress. The feedback given to each individual student can be differentiated as needed. It may become apparent that some students don't understand what the directions in the checklist mean. At that point, the teacher can decide what additional information or instruction individual students need to master the target skills. For example, a student who struggles to write a comparison/contrast paragraph in which he shows the similarities and the differences between two countries may need to use a Venn diagram as a graphic organizer. Completing this visual exercise will help the student move from the lowest level of Bloom's Taxonomy—knowledge—to the higher and more abstract level of analysis. All students need to meet the standard as the final outcome, but they may take different roads and arrive at the final destination at different times.

How Can Checklists Help Struggling Learners?

There are many reasons that struggling students need the scaffolding provided by checklists to guide them through each step of a process. They may not have paid attention during the whole-class instruction, they may have been absent (physically or mentally) during direct instruction, or they may be unorganized and not know where to start. When working with struggling learners, teachers should ask themselves: "Have I diagnosed the student's learning strengths and weaknesses?" "Is the student ready for this?" and "How can I provide more structure to help the student?" Vatterott (2009) believes that providing structure or scaffolding can help struggling students and English language learners feel they can do the job without frustration. In addition, answering the questions on a checklist does not require much writing, and many struggling students find writing tedious because they have poor fine-motor skills.

Lougy, DeRuvo, and Rosenthal (2007) discuss how a student with attention-deficit/hyperactivity disorder (ADHD) may not listen carefully to instructions and may have difficulty completing a task. The student may listen only to the first part of the directions and then begin the task impulsively before hearing the rest of the directions. Or the student may begin paying attention during the last part of the directions but have missed the instructions about how to get started. Either way, the student will become confused or frustrated because he or she cannot complete the assignment as directed. These children also have difficulty sustaining attention when it comes to planning tasks. According to Lougy et al. (2007, p. 14), "they often lack age-appropriate organizational skills to help them sequence the steps needed to complete a task, often leaving them unable to even begin a project without outside support to help them."

Teachers know that many students who have not been diagnosed with ADHD do not pay attention to directions, begin to work impulsively without waiting for directions, and get confused and frustrated when they don't know what to do. They may encounter problems approaching tasks systematically, or they may have trouble pacing themselves to accomplish tasks in the allotted time frame. They may have short attention spans or short interest spans unless they have concrete scaffolding, ongoing feedback, and frequent and immediate support.

Students who have not developed "temporal orientation" are also helped by checklists. Garner (2007, p. 102) explains that

> temporal orientation is a cognitive structure for processing information by comparing events in relationship to *when* they occur. This involves the critical skill of telling time and much more. It is essential for planning, organizing, communicating, and record keeping. . . . It is also important for studying content areas because students learn how to make connections and find patterns.

Many students need help finding patterns, and they need to see some examples provided by the teacher. Garner (2008) says that "when presented with an unfamiliar task, students without temporal orientation are often confused about where to start because they cannot plan ahead or systematically sequence their actions" (pp. 37–38). Since they are not able to determine the logical order of steps in a process, they become frustrated or lose interest. Checklists help students learn how to start, continue, and finish a task. By developing this cognitive structure and practicing it in the classroom, students establish a pattern to help them plan, organize, and communicate ideas. Once the pattern and the thinking process become a part of students' cognitive and metacognitive strategies, they begin to master tasks without any support system because they have internalized the process.

What Are Some Other Examples of Student Checklists?

The rest of this chapter will be devoted to examples of checklists from different content areas. Figure 5.3 (page 84) is a student checklist that integrates standards from several areas. The assignment that the checklist describes asks middle school students to write a letter to the editor of a newspaper and use diagrams and charts to explain to the readers how moisture affects weather. The targeted science standard relates to weather conditions, but to complete the task, students need to address standards related to letter writing, research and technology, the writing process, and conventions.

Letter-to-the-Editor Checklist for Science Performance Task

Science standard: The student explains how local weather conditions are related to the temperature, pressure, and water content of the atmosphere and the proximity to a large body of water.

Language arts standards: The student produces a letter that engages the reader; creates an organizing structure appropriate to the purpose, audience, and context; and develops the topic using supporting details.

Research and technology standard: The student uses appropriate technology to research scientific information.

Writing process standard: The student uses the writing process to brainstorm, write, rewrite, and proofread his or her letter.

Conventions standard: The student corrects his or her work and checks for correct spelling, capitalization, and punctuation.

Performance task: Write a letter to the editor of a local newspaper to explain to the readers how moisture affects weather.	Not Yet 0	Yes 1
Accuracy of information: Did you . . .		
Include 2 facts? _____ and _____		
Include 2 statistics? _____ and _____		
Use 1 quote? _____		
Organization: Did you . . .		
Engage your reader?		
Write clear topic sentences?		
Write 3 support sentences to provide evidence?		
Provide a clear focus in your paragraphs?		
Provide a satisfying closure to your letter?		

Figure 5.3: Checklist for middle school science performance task.

	Not Yet 0	Yes 1
Usage: Did you check for . . .		
Correct grammar?		
Subject/verb agreement?		
A variety of sentence structures?		
Appropriate transitions?		
Mechanics: Did you check for correct . . .		
Capitalization?		
Spelling?		
Punctuation?		
Content: Did you include . . .		
2 examples of weather patterns (for example, cold front)? _____ and _____		
2 examples of weather events (for example, tornado)? _____ and _____		
Accurate research on evaporation and weather?		
Charts, graphs, and diagrams: Did you . . .		
Include 2 visuals (for example, 1 chart/1 diagram)? _____ and _____		
Explain visuals clearly and accurately?		
Make your visuals easy to read?		
Make your visuals easy to understand?		
Present accurate information in the visuals?		

continued on next page →

	Not Yet 0	Yes 1
Letter format: Did you include . . .		
The date?		
An appropriate salutation?		
A closing?		
Your signature?		

Student Comment:

Total Points: _____ (out of 26)

23–26 = A (90%)

21–22 = B (80%)   Grade: _____

Teacher Comment:

18–20 = C (70%)

17 or under = Not Yet!

Created by Tracy Boyles, Ashley Kirby, and John Christian Cali; Cobb County School District; Marietta, Georgia. Used with permission.

A checklist for eighth-grade mathematics, shown in figure 5.4, walks students through a step-by-step process to graph linear equations and inequalities. Even though the mathematics teachers may have explained and modeled each step of the process in class, students may forget a step when they are doing homework at home. The checklist can remind them of steps and can help their parents ask them questions, even if they are not able to help with the answer.

Graphing Linear Equations Using Slope-Intercept Form

Mathematics standard: Students will graph and analyze graphs of linear equations and inequalities.

Criteria/Performance Indicators	Not Yet 0	Yes 1
Format the equation:		
• Is the equation in slope-intercept form ($y = mx + b$)? If yes, continue to the next section. If no, rewrite the equation:		

Figure 5.4: Checklist for grade-8 mathematics.

	Not Yet 0	Yes 1
● Is the y-term isolated on the left side of the equation?		
● Is the x-term after the equal symbol and in front of the constant?		
Calculate the intercepts:		
● What is your equation? _____		
● Calculate the x-intercept:		
● Did you substitute 0 into the equation in the place of y?		
● Did you calculate the value for x using the order of operations and the integer rules?		
● Did you write the x-intercept as an ordered pair?		
● In your ordered pair, is the x-intercept value you found written first, where the x-coordinate belongs?		
● In your ordered pair, is 0 written second for the y-coordinate?		
● What is the x-intercept? _____		
● Calculate the y-intercept:		
● Did you substitute 0 into the equation in the place of x? —Why do you substitute 0 in the place of x? _____		
● Did you calculate the value for y using the order of operations and the integer rules?		
● Did you write the y-intercept as an ordered pair?		
● In your ordered pair, is 0 written first for the x-coordinate?		
● In your ordered pair, is the y-intercept value you found written second, where the y-coordinate belongs?		
● What is the y-intercept? _____		

continued on next page →

	Not Yet 0	Yes 1
Construct the graph:		
● Did you begin by plotting the *y*-intercept?		
● Did you plot the slope by starting at the *y*-intercept and moving up or down for the *y*-change, and then moving right or left for the *x*-change? $$\text{Slope} = \frac{\text{Rise}}{\text{Run}} \text{ or } \frac{\text{y-change}}{\text{x-change}}; \ m = \frac{y_2 - y_1}{x_2 - x_1}$$		
● Did you plot the *x*-intercept on the *x*-axis?		
● Did you plot the *y*-intercept on the *y*-axis?		
● Did you connect the *x*- and *y*-intercepts with a solid line?		
● Did you extend your line to cover the entire coordinate plane?		
● Did you add arrows to both ends of the line?		

Created by Brenda Foyle and Sean Parker; Coweta County School System; Newnan, Georgia. Used with permission.

An assignment for a fourth-grade unit on the water cycle requires students to write a story, using pictures and key vocabulary words, about their lives as "water drops." The checklist shown in figure 5.5 provides questions to guide students through the story-writing process.

You Are a Water Drop . . . Tell Your Story
Student Checklist

Task: Write a story about your life as a "water drop" using pictures and key vocabulary words.	Not Yet 0	Yes 1
Organization		
● Do you have a title?		
● Did you include facts and details about the water cycle?		

Figure 5.5: Checklist for grade-4 unit on water cycle.

	Not Yet 0	Yes 1
● Did you stay on the topic?		
● Does your story include a clear understanding of the water cycle?		
● Did you use paragraphs to show the parts of your story?		
Vocabulary		
● Did you use these words from the vocabulary list? (evaporation, precipitation, condensation, solid, liquid, gas)		
● Did you use the scientific words correctly?		
Conventions		
● Did you use correct spelling?		
● Did you use correct capitalization?		
● Did you use correct punctuation?		
● Did you use neat handwriting?		
Illustrations		
● Does your illustration match your story?		
● Is it in the correct sequence to follow the story?		
● Is your illustration colorful?		
● Does your illustration show a clear understanding of the water cycle?		
● Does your illustration have a title?		

Created by Carrie Bette-Duncan, Scherry Lewis, Barbara Michalove, Halley Page, and Claire Smith; Clarke County School District; Athens, Georgia. Used with permission.

The fourth-grade water cycle unit also includes a group project: building a classroom terrarium. When students work in groups, they often argue or misbehave because they are not sure what they are supposed to do. Providing a checklist for group projects both keeps students focused on their task and reinforces the social skills they need to interact appropriately. The checklist in figure 5.6 (page 90) includes questions not only about building the terrarium and keeping a log but also about cooperating with others using social skills. Since collaboration is a critical skill for survival in fourth grade as well as in life, students need to learn to self-assess how their group functions as a team.

Build a Classroom Terrarium
Group Checklist

Task: Build a classroom terrarium that demonstrates your knowledge of the water cycle. Keep detailed notes/log about the environment in the terrarium.	Not Yet 0	Yes 1
Construction of project		
● Did you follow the directions?		
● Did you complete the project?		
Log entries		
● Did you observe the water cycle?		
● Did you record your data?		
● Did you use the science vocabulary?		
● Did you write in complete sentences?		
● Do your sentences start with a capital letter?		
● Do your sentences have end punctuation?		
● Did you complete your log by the due date?		
Social skills		
● Did you stay on task?		
● Did you use care with the materials?		
● Did you contribute to the group work?		
● Did you respect the opinions of the members in your group?		

Figure 5.6: Checklist for grade-4 group project.

	Not Yet 0	Yes 1
● Did you take turns to build the terrarium?		
● Did you complete your project in the allotted time?		
Student Comment: Teacher Comment:		

Created by Carrie Bette-Duncan, Scherry Lewis, Barbara Michalove, Halley Page, and Claire Smith; Clarke County School District; Athens, Georgia. Used with permission.

As we have seen, most checklists are created to help students complete a specific assignment. The checklist in figure 5.7 is different: it is a generic problem-solving checklist.

Problem-Solving Checklist

Standard: Students will develop a process to solve problems.

Assignment: Self-assess your problem-solving ability using this checklist.	Not Yet 0	Yes 1
Identification of problem: Did you . . .		
● Identify important information? Give one example:		
● Analyze data to find the real problem? What is the real problem?		
● Clarify the problem in your own words? Write a sentence to explain the problem.		
Prior knowledge: Did you . . .		
● Think about similar problems? Name one:		

Figure 5.7: Generic problem-solving checklist.

continued on next page →

	Not Yet 0	Yes 1
● Identify the knowledge you will need? List it:		
● Identify the skills you will need? Name them:		
Brainstorming possible solutions: Did you . . .		
● Select the best solution? What is it?		
● Adjust the solution as needed? How?		
● Propose alternative strategies? Give one:		
Evaluation of solution: Did you . . .		
● Collect data to document the effectiveness of the solution? What data?		
● Solve the problem? Describe how:		
● Understand the relationship between the problem and the solution? Explain:		
Transfer of problem-solving process: Can you . . .		
● Solve similar problems in the future? Predict another similar problem:		
● Solve problems independently and consistently? Self-assess your problem-solving ability:		
● Predict potential sources of problems? Explain one:		

By leaving blanks on either the content-specific or the generic checklist and requiring students to write in their answers, teachers can monitor students' progress throughout the learning process and offer specific feedback to students who are having problems. They can also stop the lesson and review or reteach the skills as needed if the whole class is experiencing problems in one or more sections. Some teachers make a poster of the generic checklist and hang it in the room to serve as a visual reminder of the steps that are involved in carefully identifying, analyzing, and solving problems. Teachers use the poster as a teaching tool, and students receive individual copies to help them remember the steps. The goal of all learning is to have students internalize the process so that they can apply it in different situations as needed. This transfer of knowledge represents one of the highest levels of learning.

Final Thoughts

The checklist is a valuable tool for performance-based learning. Checklists are not as familiar to teachers as rubrics. But they clearly have many benefits for both teachers and students. Checklists help students organize their thoughts, begin a project, follow directions, and complete all the steps. They are also malleable assessment tools. They can serve as formative assessments to provide specific, ongoing feedback to help students and teachers improve. They can serve as summative assessments to determine whether or not students have met the standards.

Benefits of Checklists

Checklists . . .

1 Provide feedback to students in real time

2 Chunk the criteria into more manageable subskills

3 Sequence the steps into logical building blocks

4 Embed the vocabulary and concepts from the language of the standards

5 "Begin with the end in mind" so that the standard is always the target

6 Build developmentally appropriate instruction

7 Reinforce the oral instructions of the teacher

8 Help parents monitor their children's homework

9 Allow students to self-assess their own work and complete do-overs

10 Encourage students to adjust their learning and improve their final products

11 Provide more accurate and consistent grades and prevent arguments such as "Why did I get a C?"

12 Help students become more independent learners

13 Help students become resources for other students by offering peer support

14 Help improve teaching and learning

15 Provide interventions for struggling students

16 Reduce classroom management problems

Checklists provide some evidence that students attempted a performance task. They show that the students followed the directions and tried to fulfill the task requirements. If the assignment focused on a less important curriculum goal or standard, the teacher could use the checklist as a summative assessment and record the final grade. In that case, the teacher would assign one point for every "Yes" or "Some Evidence" rating and a zero for every "Not Yet" or "No" rating and use the scale to determine the final grade. More often, however, checklists are used as a formative instructional and assessment tool that prepares students for the summative assessment that leads to the final evaluation. They are either not graded at all or become a factor in a grade for class participation, progress, process, or effort. Much as a teacher keeps track of practice problems, rough drafts, rehearsals, and homework, the teacher regards the checklist as a work in progress that provides a portrait of the student as a learner.

Checklists may provide valuable feedback in the formative assessment cycle regarding whether students are on target to meet the standards, but they do not describe the quality (or lack of quality) of the work. *Rubrics* lead the way in providing more descriptive feedback and specific ratings as students and teachers move into the summative assessment cycle. The next chapter will focus on the importance of converting some checklists into rubrics to give students another level of feedback and guidelines for meeting and exceeding standards by producing high-quality work.

Concluding Exercises

Reflections on Checklists

1 Why could a checklist also be called a "learning progression" or a "progress map"?

2 How do checklists provide scaffolding for struggling learners?

3 How can checklists help gifted students work independently to complete a task?

4 How can checklists be used for both formative and summative assessment?

5 When is it necessary to use both a checklist and a rubric to assess student work?

Action Steps

List three action steps you plan to take to include more checklists in your assessment repertoire.

Step 1:

Step 2:

Step 3:

6

Rubrics: All Roads Lead to the Standards

Rubrics provide criterion-based scoring procedures that guide teachers' instruction and help them evaluate students' performances more objectively. It takes skill and practice to create rubrics, but when they are done right, "rubrics are our friends!"

What Are Rubrics?

Defined in the simplest terms, a rubric is a scoring guide used to evaluate students' responses to a performance assessment. Popham (1999) says that a rubric has three important features:

- *Evaluative criteria.* These are the factors to be used in determining the quality of a student's response.

- *Descriptions of qualitative differences for the evaluative criteria.* For each evaluative criterion, a description must be supplied so that qualitative distinctions in students' responses can be made using the criterion.

- *An indication of whether a holistic or analytical approach is to be used.* The rubric must indicate whether the evaluative criteria are to be applied collectively in the form of *holistic* scoring or on a criterion-by-criterion basis in the form of *analytical* scoring. (p. 167)

Rubrics enable teachers to distinguish between different levels of quality in performances and products. Solomon (1998) notes that rubrics should be based on the "results of stated performance standards and be composed of scaled descriptive levels of progress toward the result" (p. 120). The descriptors for the different levels should specifically match the task and incorporate as much of the language of the standards (LOTS) and benchmarks as possible. Checklists support student learning by describing the criteria that make up a standard and helping students keep track of whether they have attempted to meet them. Rubrics extend checklists by describing the different levels of quality that can be achieved on each evaluative criterion.

How Are Rubrics Structured?

Rubrics help teachers make a valid inference about a student's mastery of a specific skill in a performance. Popham (1999) points out that "skill-focused" rubrics can also be used to guide a teacher's instructional planning. For example, the evaluative criteria for judging the organization of a student's narrative essay could state:

> Two aspects of organization will be employed in the appraisal of students' narrative essays—namely, *overall structure* and *sequence*. To earn maximum credit, an essay must embody an overall structure containing an introduction, a body, and a conclusion. The content of the body of the essay must be sequenced in a reasonable manner—for instance, in a chronological, logical, or order-of-importance sequence. (Popham, 1999, p. 250)

Figure 6.1 shows one criterion from a skill-focused rubric for writing a persuasive essay: writing an effective thesis statement. A checklist would simply ask a student whether or not he or she wrote a thesis statement. The rubric asks the student to examine the thesis statement he or she has attempted to write and provides a roadmap for building it from a basic sentence to a powerful thesis statement designed to persuade all readers to agree with the author's beliefs. The rubric provides descriptors for four successive levels of quality and assigns a numeric score as well as a student-friendly label to each one. At level 1, a student can write a sentence that describes the main idea of the paper; at level 4, a student can write a thesis statement that not only describes the main idea of the paper but also introduces the three controlling ideas that will be explained in three paragraphs of the body of the essay. The level-4 thesis statement provides an overview of the persuasive arguments that will be used to make the writer's case. Students self-assess where they are on the continuum and take steps to strengthen their thesis statements by adding the necessary elements to reach their goals.

Criterion	Extra Homework 1	Teacher's Aide 2	English Teacher 3	Nobel Prize for Literature 4	Score
The student can write an effective thesis statement.	The student can write a sentence that introduces the topic.	The student can write a thesis statement that introduces *one* controlling idea that will be addressed in one paragraph in the body of the essay.	The student can write a thesis statement that introduces *two* controlling ideas that will be addressed in two paragraphs in the body of the essay.	The student can write a thesis statement that introduces *three* controlling ideas that will be addressed in three paragraphs in the body of the essay.	

Figure 6.1: Rubric for thesis statement criterion.

Writing an effective thesis statement is only one of perhaps ten to fifteen criteria specified by the persuasive essay standard. A rubric that includes all the criteria for the standard, provides descriptors for each criterion, and scores each one separately is considered an "analytical rubric." Analytical rubrics are often referred to as "teaching rubrics" because they provide specific feedback that pinpoints students' strengths and weaknesses in all aspects of a performance task. Analytical rubrics are critical components of formative classroom assessment, providing guidance "real fast" and in "real time" so that students can improve their work. Students are able to "do over" any criterion by following the descriptors that tell them exactly what they need to do to move from a 1 or a 2 on the rubric to a 3 or a 4. Most importantly, students can assess their own work immediately, without waiting for the teacher's input, and can work at their own pace to complete the task.

A teacher may use either an analytical or a holistic scoring strategy to assign a grade for a task such as writing a persuasive essay. Popham (2006, p. 240) explains that "an analytical strategy requires the scorer to render criterion-by-criterion scores that may or may not ultimately be aggregated into an overall score." *Holistic*, on the other hand, means that the integrated whole has a reality independent of and greater than the sum of its parts. Therefore, instead of focusing on and giving a separate score for each criterion, the teacher reviews the entire work and assigns one score (1, 2, 3, or 4) that summarizes the overall quality of the work. Figure 6.2 (page 98) is an example of a holistic rubric for writing a persuasive essay. (The complete analytical rubric for the persuasive essay appears in figure 6.11, page 112.)

A holistic score reflects a general classification of a student's work, but it does not provide feedback on any specific criterion. Guskey and Bailey (2001, p. 32) point out that "students seeking ways to improve their achievement or performance get little direction from holistic scoring, just as they get little guidance from a single grade written at the top of their paper. To make improvements, they need detailed and analytical information paired with specific suggestions for correction." Teachers sometimes use holistic rubrics for summative work required at the end of a marking period, when it is too late to give feedback or allow students another do-over before final grades are due. Statewide assessments are usually graded holistically by several trained evaluators who each assign one grade and arrive at consensus about the final score, sometimes with the help of an additional evaluator. They base their decisions on their training and their review of various anchor papers representing different attributes and scores.

What Are the Criteria for Good Rubrics?

One of the challenges of using rubrics for grading formative and summative assessments is that systems for scoring can be inconsistent. Some districts require teachers to give students a 4 on the rubric if they meet state standards. Other districts require teachers to give students a 3 if they meet the standards and a 4 if they exceed the standards. Sometimes teachers at the same grade level and at the same school use different methods to determine scores. Therefore, students who do the same quality of work could receive a 3 or a B from one teacher and a 4 or an A from the teacher right across the hall. Such inconsistency in grading procedures takes the objectivity out of the rubric.

The trend seems to be to use the score of 4 to indicate that a student has exceeded the standard by doing exceptional work consistently and independently. As mentioned earlier, one way of differentiating learning is to extend assignments to challenge students who may be able to meet the standards on their first try. These exceptional students should have to stretch themselves and add to their knowledge base to demonstrate progress, and the rubric should include a level that reflects that.

Holistic Rubric for a Persuasive Essay

4	• Organizing structure clearly supports writer's position. • Creative opening (hook, lead) grabs the reader's attention. • Thesis statement clearly identifies writer's position and three main points to support position. • Essay uses concrete and descriptive words. • Writer's position is effectively restated for closure at beginning of last paragraph. • All irrelevant and extraneous details have been deleted. • Essay contains no mechanical errors.
3	• Organizing structure helps paper flow naturally. • Opening (hook, lead) gets the reader's attention. • Thesis statement identifies writer's position but does not list the points to be made. • Essay uses some concrete and descriptive words. • Writer's position is restated within the first two sentences of last paragraph for closure. • Most irrelevant and extraneous details have been deleted. • Essay contains one or two mechanical errors.
2	• Organizing structure was attempted but lacks coherence. • Opening (hook, lead) is not clearly related to the topic. • Thesis statement lists points to be made but does not identify topic or position. • Essay rarely uses concrete and descriptive words. • Writer's position is restated near the end of closing paragraph. • Some irrelevant and extraneous details have been deleted. • Essay contains three to five mechanical errors.
1	• No recognizable organizing structure. • No opening (hook, lead) to engage reader. • Thesis statement does not identify topic, position, or main points. • No use of concrete and descriptive words. • No closure; the paper just ends. • Irrelevant and extraneous details have not been deleted. • Essay contains six or more mechanical errors.

Adapted from Persuasive Essay Analytical Rubric, created by Marva Bell, Lori Higgs, LaKeia King, and Shanon Melson; Carrollton City Schools; Carrollton, Georgia. Used with permission.

Figure 6.2: Holistic rubric for persuasive essay.

Once teachers on a team have worked together to create a checklist, as described in chapter 5, the next step is to construct a rubric together so that they agree on the guidelines for the scoring system. The checklist in figure 6.3 can help the teams by showing them the criteria for informative rubrics and allowing them to assess the rubrics they create. This checklist can be adapted to fit district and school requirements. The important thing is for the teams to engage in meaningful conversations to make sure that everyone understands the reasons for the criteria, the terminology associated with the criteria, and the rationale for weighting some criteria more than others (see the following section). Once members of the community of assessors agree on the structure of the rubrics, they need to be consistent in the creation of all their rubrics. The consistency of the rubric structure helps ensure more validity and reliability throughout the grade level, content area, school, and district.

Guidelines for Constructing Rubrics

Assignment: Self-assess your rubric using these guidelines.	Not Yet 0	Yes 1
Alignment to standards: Did you . . .		
Use the language of the standards?		
List key events, people, and concepts?		
Correlate the rubric to course goals and objectives?		
Evaluative criteria: Did you . . .		
Link the criteria to the categories in the standards and the checklists created for the students?		
List the criteria in the left-hand column?		
Chunk the big categories in sequential order, list them in bold, and place them in shaded rows that are not rated or scored?		
List subskills as bullet points under each category?		
Descriptors of criteria: Did you . . .		
Describe each increment of progress toward goals?		
Avoid gaps or overlapping descriptors between levels?		
Use clear and concise descriptions of quality work?		

Figure 6.3: Checklist for assessing a rubric.

continued on next page →

	Not Yet 0	Yes 1
● Focus on observable behaviors and performances?		
● Use pictures for visual appeal?		
Scoring: Did you . . .		
● Label levels using a combination of numbers, words, or pictures?		
● Use a range from 1 to 4 with graduated steps of quality?		
● Provide clear expectations for students at each level?		
● Create a scale to convert the rubric score to a letter or number grade (for example, 18–20 points = 90% = A)?		
● Weight the rubric to emphasize important criteria from standards or goals for the week?		

Total Points: _____ (out of 17)

Scale

15–17 points = Your rubric rocks! (90%) = A

13–14 points = Review your rubric! (80%) = B

12 or below = The rubric police are coming! (70%) = C

Reflections on my rubric:

My new goals:

Signature: _____   Date: _____

What Is a Weighted Rubric?

Most rubrics include a column on the right-hand side for recording a score for the student's performance on each evaluative criterion. The score is usually the same as the level the student achieves on the criterion. For example, in figure 6.1 (page 96), a student who has written a level-3 thesis statement will receive a score of 3 on that criterion.

Many times, however, teachers consider some criteria in a rubric to be more instructionally critical than others. In these cases, it is possible to *weight* the criteria to reflect their relative importance. The mechanism for doing so is to designate a multiplier for the score for each criterion. The multiplier is displayed in the "Score" column, so that the teacher writes in the initial score (level achieved), multiplies it, and arrives at the weighted score. The score column also indicates the maximum number of points possible on each criterion (shown in parentheses under the equation for the weighted score). Figure 6.4 shows how the criterion from figure 6.1 might be weighted. (See fig. 6.11, page 112, for an example of a complete weighted rubric for a persuasive essay.)

Criterion	Extra Homework 1	Teacher's Aide 2	English Teacher 3	Nobel Prize for Literature 4	Score
The student can write an effective thesis statement.	The student can write a sentence that introduces the topic.	The student can write a thesis statement that introduces *one* controlling idea that will be addressed in one paragraph in the body of the essay.	The student can write a thesis statement that introduces *two* controlling ideas that will be addressed in two paragraphs in the body of the essay.	The student can write a thesis statement that introduces *three* controlling ideas that will be addressed in three paragraphs in the body of the essay.	____ x 3 = ____ (12)

Figure 6.4: A weighted criterion.

Teachers might decide to give a criterion more weight for any of the following reasons:

- It relates to one or more critical learning standards.
- It is the focus of the lesson that week.
- It represents an important skill or concept needed for future learning.
- It targets an important objective or learning goal for the unit.
- It targets a key skill that will be assessed on standardized tests.

Criteria that are part of the task but not considered as critical as other criteria can be given less weight. Students writing a science report might have their score on "knowledge of scientific concepts" or "problem-solving skills" weighted five or six times and their score on "mechanics" weighted only two times. Spelling, punctuation, and capitalization count toward the final grade, but the science teacher focuses more on the students' ability to meet science standards than their ability to use mechanics appropriately.

Teachers determine when and how they will weight scores on a rubric. The rubric for writing a persuasive essay could vary from day to day or week to week, depending on what the lesson emphasizes. If a teacher spends three days focusing on grammar and usage, the rubric for that week could weight that criterion more heavily than the criterion for organization or research because it is the week's target instructional goal. "Visual appeal" and "neatness" can be included in the grade, but they should not be given the same weight as the more substantive performance and thinking skills assessed in the rubric.

How Can Rigor Be Added to Rubrics?

Since the word *standard* seems almost commonplace, educators have to show students how they can transcend standard work and constantly strive to improve their performance. In most cases, teachers review the state standard and write the descriptors for *meeting* the standard in the level-3 column. They then go backwards and fill in the descriptors for level 2, which indicates that a student is making progress toward or approaching meeting the standard, and then provide desciptors for level 1, which indicates that a student is a novice who will need intensive interventions. The descriptors for a score of 4 ("Exceeds the Standard" or "Exceeds Expectations") on a rubric can challenge students to extend their knowledge and skills. Students do not have to meet all the criteria to receive a 4, but they should be able to meet several of them.

Figure 6.5 shows how teachers can add rigor to rubrics by making a score of 4 represent not only exceptional performance but also exceptional thinking. Sternberg (2007/2008) suggests that teachers should teach students to think analytically, creatively, practically, and wisely and should give them frequent opportunities to demonstrate these different kinds of thinking. Students who earn a 4 on their rubrics should be able to go beyond mastering the skills and demonstrate their ability to think critically and creatively, to self-assess the feasibility of their proposals, to grasp the big ideas, and to develop the enduring understandings that will transfer to life beyond school.

Introducing the "rigorous rubric" early in the year will focus students on the ultimate goals of the learning experience. It will also help them realize "how good is good enough" and how exceptional one has to be to exceed the standards and achieve deep understanding of important concepts. The criteria in level 4 will generate discussion throughout the instructional process. Sometimes students will want teachers to be more prescriptive so that they will know if they are doing what is needed to earn a high grade. Students might want to know what it means to be "original and creative." The teacher might suggest that if he or she tells them what original work looks like, it might not be original anymore. Students don't like ambiguity, but sometimes they need to discover for themselves the meaning of these terms and go outside the box to achieve intellectual independence.

Standard: _____

| Criterion

The student can . . . | 1

Below the Standard | 2

Approaching the Standard | 3

Meets the Standard | 4

Exceeds the Standard

Can the student . . . . | Score |
|---|---|---|---|---|---|
| | | | | ☐ Meet the criteria consistently and independently? | |
| | | | | ☐ Teach other students by explaining the process clearly and logically? | |
| | | | | ☐ Answer all the essential questions that framed the unit? | |
| | | | | ☐ Grasp the big ideas or key concepts of the standards? | |
| | | | | ☐ Use creative ideas that are original and compelling? | |
| | | | | ☐ Use thoughtful decision-making strategies? | |
| | | | | ☐ Apply both critical and creative problem-solving skills? | |
| | | | | ☐ Provide practical responses that are feasible? | |
| | | | | ☐ Use analytical responses (balanced, logical, and organized)? | |

Figure 6.5: How to add rigor to rubrics.

How Can Rubrics Assess Thinking Skills?

In addition to adding rigor to rubrics by including thinking skills in the level-4 descriptors, teachers should create rubrics that help students learn how to *improve* their thinking skills. When teachers make the criteria explicit, students will learn how to classify each thinking skill, label it appropriately when they use it, assess their use of it, and be able to use it in other situations. Being able to think "metacognitively" is essential for learning.

Figure 6.6 is a rubric to assess students' ability to draw conclusions from their reading. The left column highlights the main criteria. Several of the descriptors for the various levels are very specific, whereas others allow more choice. Note that the criterion of "uses thinking skills" lists four thinking skills: predicting, summarizing, analyzing, and evaluating. The rubric does not state which skill would be considered the lowest level, or a 1 score, nor does it say which skill would rate a 4. The purpose of the levels for this criterion is not to rank-order the skills, but instead to show the number of thinking skills students are able to use appropriately.

Figure 6.7 (page 106) shows a rubric for assessing thinking skills in which the descriptors have not been filled in. Sometimes students themselves should be able to describe what they believe are escalating levels of quality ranging from 1 to 4. Once students can label their own thinking, they are better able to use it appropriately when needed. By creating their own descriptors for each criterion, they demonstrate that they have internalized the thinking process and that they can differentiate the exceptional use of thinking skills from an inadequate or average use of thinking skills. Vagle (2009) says that involving students in their own learning is a key characteristic of assessment that has yielded positive results. Students should be able to move beyond relying on the teacher to supply all the descriptors of quality because they need to learn how to generate and internalize their own criteria for excellence as they go through life.

How Can Checklists Be Converted Into Rubrics?

If teams of teachers work together to create student checklists for major projects and performances, they can convert those checklists into rubrics quickly and easily. The first step is to change the questions in the checklist into phrases or short sentences. For example, if the checklist contains the question "Did you write a thesis statement to introduce your main idea?" the rubric could change that into a short declarative sentence such as "The student can write an effective thesis statement" or a phrase such as "thesis statement." If students are not sure what "thesis statement" means, they can refer to their checklist to see the context. The rubric should contain the same criteria as the checklist, but in a shortened form.

The next step is to designate the four ratings for the rubric, in contrast to the two ratings for the checklist. The checklist ratings show only whether the student has attempted to meet a criterion. The rubric ratings show increments of quality, increasing to the highest level of 4 to indicate exceeding expectations or standards. The ratings can be phrased in terms of performance on the standard (below, approaching, meets, exceeds) or can be worded humorously to make the rubric more student-friendly.

The next step is to write the detailed descriptors for each level. When rubrics are used for formative assessment, the descriptors help students improve their work. When it is time for a summative assessment, the descriptors help teachers make a final judgment.

Criterion The student can . . .	1 Below the Standard	2 Approaching the Standard	3 Meets the Standard	4 Exceeds the Standard	Score
Retell the story	Retells information about the main characters	Retells information about the main characters, the setting, and the problem	Retells information about the main characters, the setting, the problem, the theme, and the conclusion	Retells the entire story using accurate details arranged in sequential order	
Identify the problem	Cannot find the problem	Identifies a minor problem	Identifies the real problem	Identifies and explains the real problem and links it to prior knowledge	
Identify the solution	Identifies incorrect solution	Identifies one solution, but not the most logical one	Identifies the most logical and appropriate solution	Uses details and descriptions to identify and explain the most logical and appropriate solution	
Use details to draw conclusion	Does not use details to draw conclusion	Uses one accurate detail to support conclusion	Uses two accurate details to support conclusion	Uses three or more accurate details to support conclusion convincingly	
Use thinking skills (predicting, summarizing, analyzing, evaluating)	Uses one thinking skill effectively	Uses two thinking skills effectively	Uses three thinking skills effectively	Uses four thinking skills effectively	
Use problem-solving skills	Misses the real problem	Identifies the real problem	Brainstorms possible solutions to problems	Evaluates the effectiveness of the solutions independently	

Figure 6.6: Rubric to assess students' ability to draw conclusions from reading.

Standard: _____

Assignment: _____

Thinking Skill	1 Below the Standard	2 Approaching the Standard	3 Meets the Standard	4 Exceeds the Standard	Score
Decision making					
● Gathering data ● Examining data ● Analyzing data					
Prioritizing					
● Creating criteria ● Ranking criteria ● Justifying ranking of criteria					
Predicting					
● Using prior knowledge ● Using visual and graphic clues ● Using vocabulary ● Using imagination					
Sequencing					
● Listing steps ● Arranging steps in order ● Evaluating the order of the steps					
Comparing					
● Identifying characteristics ● Identifying similarities between the characteristics					

Figure 6.7: Rubric for assessing thinking skills (students provide descriptors).

Thinking Skill	1 Below the Standard	2 Approaching the Standard	3 Meets the Standard	4 Exceeds the Standard	Score
Contrasting					
• Identifying characteristics • Identifying differences between the characteristics					

The final step is to weight the criteria. Every criterion on a checklist will receive a score of either 0 or 1, regardless of its importance. Rubrics are often weighted to focus on the important concepts or criteria, because they represent the curricular goals of the unit. In a checklist, neatness is given the same weight as understanding of key concepts. In a rubric, neatness and following directions may count for a maximum of four points, but understanding of key concepts, organization, and research could all be weighted five, six, or seven times to indicate their importance.

When converting checklists into rubrics, teachers should keep these major differences in mind:

1 Checklists use an interrogative format to present the criteria, whereas rubrics state them with a word, short phrase, or declarative sentence.

2 Checklists require students to write some of their answers to show they have completed a step, whereas rubrics require students to circle or check one of the prewritten descriptors.

3 Checklists may be used as summative assessments if teachers feel the task and standard were not important enough to warrant a rubric, but they are more often used as formative assessments that provide feedback and are not graded. Rubrics may be used as formative assessments for practice, but they often become summative assessments for the final grade.

4 Checklists may have a point value attached to providing an answer (usually a 0 or a 1) and a scale for the purpose of feedback only, whereas a rubric almost always has a point value and a scale to determine a final percentage or letter grade.

5 Checklists count each "Yes" or "Some Evidence" answer as worth one point, regardless of the criterion's importance. Rubrics, however, sometimes have weighted scores to emphasize the more important criteria, based on the standards and big ideas.

A good way to see the relationship between a checklist and a rubric is to look at a performance task for which both have been created. Figure 6.8 (page 108) presents the scenario for a fifth-grade mathematics performance task that targets the standard "Students will continue to develop their understanding of the meaning of common fractions and compute with them."

Cookie Crunch Time!

Problem scenario: *Emergency alert! Attention!* Due to the rising gas prices and budget cuts, our overnight field trip has been canceled. If we want to go on our trip, we have to raise money! Let's start with a bake sale. It has been the biggest money maker for our school in the past. We want to appeal to as many people as possible, so we will make different types of cookies: chocolate chip, oatmeal, and sugar cookies. We have three different jobs to complete. Job 1: Based on the principal's data, we need to bake three times as many chocolate chip cookies as oatmeal cookies and twice as many sugar cookies as oatmeal cookies. We only need to bake one batch of oatmeal cookies. Job 2: Using the information we gathered, we need to take the three recipes and create a shopping list. Make sure you combine like ingredients. Job 3: Rank the ingredients from the smallest amount to the largest amount. Be sure to show how you ranked the amounts. *Let's get started,* because our bake sale is next week and we must gather our information first!

Created by Louise Brockinton, Susan Cardin, Julie Hinkle, Kerstin Long, and Leah York; Clarke County School District; Athens, Georgia. Used with permission.

Figure 6.8: Grade-5 mathematics performance task.

To guide students through the task of buying the cookie ingredients for their bake sale, the teachers provide the checklist shown in figure 6.9.

Checklist for Rank-Ordered Shopping List for Bake Sale

Assignment: Rank the ingredients from the smallest amount to the largest amount. Be sure to show how you ranked the amounts.	Not Yet 0	Yes 1
Larger recipes—accuracy of multiplication computation		
● Did you multiply each ingredient in the oatmeal recipe by 2 (did you double each ingredient) to reach the ingredient amounts for sugar cookies?		
● Did you multiply each ingredient in the oatmeal recipe by 3 (did you triple each ingredient) to reach the ingredient amounts for chocolate chip cookies?		
● Did you rewrite the sugar cookie recipe?		
● Did you rewrite the chocolate chip cookie recipe?		

Figure 6.9: Checklist for grade-5 mathematics performance task.

	Not Yet 0	Yes 1
Shopping list—accuracy of addition computation		
● Did you add the amounts of flour from all three recipes? What total did you get? _____		
● Did you add the amounts of sugar from all three recipes? What total did you get? _____		
● Did you add the amounts of vanilla from all three recipes? What total did you get? _____		
● Did you add the number of eggs from all three recipes? What total did you get? _____		
● Did you add the amounts of butter or shortening from all three recipes? What total did you get? _____		
● Did you add the amounts of extra ingredients from all three recipes? What total did you get? _____		
Ranking ingredients—accuracy of comparisons of fractions		
● Did you group your amounts by the measurement tools? ● Teaspoon ingredients		
● Tablespoon ingredients		
● Cup ingredients		
● Did you rank-order the ingredients within the teaspoon ingredients from smallest to largest?		
● Did you rank-order the tablespoon ingredients from smallest to largest?		
● Did you rank-order the cup ingredients from smallest to largest?		
● Did you begin the list with the rank-ordered teaspoon ingredients list?		

continued on next page →

	Not Yet 0	Yes 1
● Did you next add to the list the rank-ordered tablespoon ingredients list?		
● Did you finish the list with the rank-ordered cup ingredients list?		

Created by Louise Brockinton, Susan Cardin, Julie Hinkle, Kerstin Long, and Leah York; Clarke County School District; Athens, Georgia. Used with permission.

Once the students have used the checklist to self-assess whether they have accomplished all the steps necessary to tabulate the correct amounts of ingredients for their bake sale, the teachers provide them with a rubric that was developed from the checklist (fig. 6.10). The rubric enables them to assess their computational abilities based on the descriptors. Students check their work and make corrections as needed to improve their scores. Teachers could use this rubric as a formative assessment to help students improve, but they could also use it as the summative assessment at the end of the fractions unit to give a final grade.

To return to an example from an earlier chapter, the checklist for the fourth- or fifth-grade persuasive essay shown in figure 1.2 (page 15) helps students write their rough draft and get organized with the writing process. Once the students feel comfortable with their progress, the teachers give them a rubric that was developed from that checklist (fig. 6.11, page 112). The rubric helps students focus on the quality of their performance on each criterion. Some teachers prefer to give students the checklist and the rubric together so that they can see immediately what they have to do to score a 4. Other teachers feel the rubric might overwhelm some of the students, especially those who are struggling. They prefer to use the checklist first, to help students get started, and to give out the rubric later, when students feel more confident in the process. Of course, some high-achieving students who want to work at their own pace will want to see the rubric immediately so that they can work independently.

Often, teachers feel that a checklist alone is enough to use for a formative assessment because it gives students an organizing structure to help them complete the project or performance, and it provides them with feedback. If the standard addressed, however, is a power standard, it is important enough to create a rubric to assess it. Since students begin writing persuasive essays in the third or fourth grade and continue to write them throughout middle school, high school, and college, the persuasive essay warrants both a checklist and a rubric. Students can check off criteria on the checklist to show that they at least attempted the work and that they are able to follow an organizational framework, but the rubric gives clear expectations for quality work and shows what is required to earn each score. Most importantly, rubrics provide feedback to students to help them self-assess their own work and decide on the next steps to take to meet and exceed expectations.

Rank-Ordered Shopping List Rubric

Mathematics standard: Students will continue to develop their understanding of the meaning of common fractions and compute with them.

Criterion	1 Insufficient Where's the Pepto?!	2 Progressing Only a few more bites to go	3 Meets the Standard Clean Plate Club	4 Exceeds the Standard I can't believe I ate the whole thing! Please, can I have more?	Score
Multiplication The student models the multiplication of common fractions *by rewriting each recipe with the new amounts of each ingredient.*	5 or more errors in computation of ingredients	3–4 errors in computation of ingredients	1–2 errors in computation of ingredients	Absolutely correct computation of all ingredients!	
Addition and subtraction The student adds and subtracts common fractions and mixed numbers with unlike denominators *by creating an accurate shopping list and combining like ingredients.*	3 or more errors in addition and subtraction of ingredients	2 errors in addition and subtraction of ingredients	1 error in addition and subtraction of ingredients	Absolutely correct addition and subtraction of all ingredients!	
Comparing fractions The student finds equivalent fractions and simplifies fractions. The student uses <, >, or = to compare fractions and justifies the comparison *by ranking the cookie ingredients from the smallest to the largest amount.*	5 or more errors in ordering of ingredients	3–4 errors in ordering of ingredients	1–2 errors in ordering of ingredients	Absolutely correct ordering of all ingredients!	

Comments: Final Grade: _____ /12

Created by Louise Brockinton, Susan Cardin, Julie Hinkle, Kerstin Long, and Leah York; Clarke County School District, Athens, Georgia. Used with permission.

Figure 6.10: Rubric for grade-5 mathematics task.

Persuasive Essay Rubric

Standard: The student demonstrates competence in writing a persuasive essay.

Criterion The student:	1 Below the Standard	2 Approaching the Standard	3 Meets the Standard	4 Exceeds the Standard	Score
Selects an organizing structure	Essay is poorly organized and difficult to follow.	Structure was attempted but lacks smooth flow.	Organizing structure allows the paper to flow naturally.	Paper is well organized throughout and structured to clearly support writer's position.	___ x 2 = ___ (8)
Engages the reader	Hook, lead, or attention grabber is missing.	Hook, lead, or attention grabber is not clearly connected to the topic.	Hook, lead, or attention grabber gets the reader's attention but may be weak.	Creative opening grabs the reader's attention. Hook, lead, or attention grabber is electrifying!	___ x 2 = ___ (8)
States a clear position	Thesis statement does not identify topic, position, or main points.	Thesis statement lists points to be discussed but does not identify topic or position.	Thesis statement clearly identifies the writer's position within the introductory paragraph but does not outline the points to be made.	Thesis statement clearly identifies the writer's position and outlines three main points to be discussed.	___ x 3 = ___ (12)
Supports a clear position	Evidence and examples are irrelevant and/or not shown to support the writer's position.	At least one piece of evidence supports the writer's position.	Most evidence and examples are specific and support the writer's position.	All evidence and examples are specific and strongly support the writer's position.	___ x 5 = ___ (20)
Addresses reader concerns	Counterarguments are neither identified nor explained.	Counterarguments are identified but not refuted.	Counterarguments are identified and somewhat refuted.	Counterarguments are identified and effectively refuted.	___ x 5 = ___ (20)
Raises the level of language	Never uses concrete and descriptive words. Very dull reading.	Rarely uses concrete and descriptive words. Somewhat dull reading.	Uses some concrete and descriptive words.	Consistently uses concrete and descriptive words. Shows a lively writer's voice.	___ x 2 = ___ (8)

Figure 6.11: Persuasive essay analytical rubric.

Criterion The student:	1 Below the Standard	2 Approaching the Standard	3 Meets the Standard	4 Exceeds the Standard	Score
Provides closure	There is no closure; the paper just ends.	The writer's position is restated within the closing paragraph, but not near the beginning of the paragraph.	The closure is recognizable; the writer's position is restated within the first two sentences of the closing paragraph.	The closure is a strong, effective restatement of the writer's position, and it begins the closing paragraph.	___ x 2 = ___ (8)
Excludes extraneous details and inappropriate information	Never deleted irrelevant and extraneous details.	Deleted some irrelevant and extraneous details.	Deleted most irrelevant and extraneous details.	Completely deleted irrelevant and extraneous details.	___ x 2 = ___ (8)
Demonstrates grasp of mechanics, usage, and grammar	Essay contains six or more consistent errors that are distracting or interfere with the reader's understanding.	Essay contains three to five errors in mechanics, usage, and grammar, but they do not distract the reader or interfere with understanding.	Essay contains one to two errors in mechanics, usage, or grammar, but they do not distract the reader or interfere with the reader's understanding.	Essay contains no errors in mechanics, usage, or grammar. Writer demonstrates a grasp of mechanics, usage, and grammar.	___ x 2 = ___ (8)

Grade Equivalents   A = 90–100 points   B = 80–89 points   C = 70–79 points   69 or Below = Do Over!

Total Points: _____ (out of 100)

Comments:

Created by Marva Bell, Lori Higgs, LaKeia King, and Shanon Melson; Carrollton City Schools; Carrollton, Georgia. Used with permission.

What Are Fun Rubrics?

If students have not used a rubric before, fun rubrics are a good way to introduce them to the *pattern* of a rubric so that they begin to understand the process of creating and using rubrics to self-assess their work. At first, students may be confused by the rubric's structure, because the criteria for the project or performance are listed on the left side (similar to the checklist), but the descriptors are arranged from left to right, starting at the lowest level of performance. Dividing students into groups and having them build fun rubrics helps them understand the elements of rubrics and internalize the process.

Building fun rubrics begins with choosing a topic that would not normally be considered ripe for assessment. It seems to be easier for students to grasp the idea of describing something at four levels of quality if they begin by thinking about a topic at its highest level, or "the perfect _____." Since all assessment should "begin with the end in mind," it is appropriate to visualize the epitome of anything and then fill in the incremental steps necessary to achieve that lofty goal. For example, if students were to write a rubric for the "perfect basketball player," they might begin at level 4 listing the attributes of Michael Jordan or LeBron James and then fill in the other levels with traits of basketball player wannabees who aspire to be NBA All-Stars.

Here are some examples of topics that can get students started:

- The perfect student
- The perfect teacher
- The perfect field trip
- The perfect after-school job
- The perfect snow day
- The perfect vacation
- The perfect lunch
- The perfect pet
- The perfect date
- The perfect principal
- The perfect rock concert
- The perfect weekend

Once students choose a topic, they can start thinking about their idealized vision for level 4 and then address each lower level of quality by choosing criteria and writing descriptors. Teachers must be sure to monitor the groups carefully for inappropriate criteria or descriptors and allow the students to share their fun rubrics with the class. The rubrics should be posted around the room so that all students have a visual reminder of what a rubric is and how it is used to assess quality.

Figure 6.12 is a partially filled-in fun rubric that teachers could use for assessing the perfect student. Descriptors have been provided for the criterion of "behavior." Teachers might fill in other criteria based on their own students or students they would like to have in a perfect world!

Fun Rubric for Assessing the Perfect Student

Criterion	Reform School-Bound! 1	The Unknown Student! 2	The Brown-Noser! 3	The Teacher's Pet! 4
Behavior	Snarls at teacher; insults fellow students; referred to in-house suspension weekly; referred to out-of-school suspension monthly	Remains in the time-out area most of the day; leaves only for counseling services and meetings with assistant principal in charge of school discipline	Smiles all the time, listens attentively, nods head approvingly, takes perfect notes in impeccable handwriting, and laughs at all the teacher's jokes	Monitors the class when the teacher leaves the room; reports students who did not behave; showers the teacher with croissants, dark chocolates, and vanilla lattes
Appearance				
Academics				
Punctuality				
Social skills				

Figure 6.12: Fun rubric for assessing the perfect student.

Figure 6.13 (page 116) provides a template for constructing fun rubrics for other topics. The blanks above the numerical ratings may be filled in with either pictures or funny phrases.

Once students have some fun creating rubrics, they begin to see the structure and patterns of real rubrics and to understand how the criteria, descriptors, and scoring work. The benefits of using rubrics to assess subjective work become clearer. Even the students will come to believe that, indeed, rubrics are our friends!

Final Thoughts

Some teachers believe that although rubrics may be our friends, they can be difficult to create, time-consuming to use, and sometimes very "unfriendly" for teachers, parents, and students. It is no wonder that many teachers may agree with the *concept* of rubrics but resist the tremendous time commitment needed to create them. The emphasis on performance-based learning, which requires that students apply what they know in authentic situations, means that today's teachers have numerous

Fun Rubric for Assessing: _____

Criterion	1	2	3	4

Figure 6.13: Fun rubric template.

projects and performances to assess. Creating rubrics for every important project or performance could be overwhelming if teachers attempted the task on their own. But when teachers work in teams to create common assessments that include performance tasks, checklists, and rubrics, they not only learn from one another, but they also share the workload and become more consistent and reliable in their instruction and assessments.

Creating original checklists and rubrics aligned to state standards is the ultimate goal, but sometimes teachers find it easier to use ready-made rubrics in textbooks, in professional development books, and on education websites. For their assessments to be valid, however, teachers will need to alter the language of the rubrics to make sure it matches their own state's standards. Rubrics obtained from a teacher's home state department of education website will use the language of the standards that will also be included on the state's high-stakes test. Rubrics from sources outside the state will have to be revised, and teachers may also need to add kid-friendly words next to the standards vocabulary to help all students understand the language of the standards.

The purpose of rubrics is to guide students through the steps they must take to improve the quality of their work. Before rubrics (B.R.), teachers had to write detailed comments on each student's paper, providing feedback, corrections, praise, and encouragement. The process was very time intensive and teacher directed. Most states now require teachers to examine student work and give each student specific feedback and goals for improvement. If teachers incorporate most of their improvement guidelines into the rubrics, it enables them to give specific feedback to *all* of their students, consistently and equitably. It is important to leave a space on each rubric for teacher commentary that offers personalized feedback and individualized goals so that students know their next steps and feel recognized by the teacher for their efforts. Because students can also use rubrics to assess their own work or to help their peers, they become an integral part of the learning process rather than passive recipients of a teacher's red marks.

Once rubrics are created, they do save time, and they shift the responsibility for directing learning from the teacher as the ultimate assessor to the student as an independent learner and critical self-assessor. After all, students need to know how to self-assess, reflect, and correct their own work if they are to become lifelong learners. The rubric starts them on the road to self-improvement. And, as everyone knows, *rubrics are our friends*, and all roads lead to the standards!

Concluding Exercises

Reflections on Rubrics

1 What are the major differences between checklists and rubrics?

2 Why should rubrics always contain the language of the standards?

3 How can rubrics help gifted students work independently to complete a task?

4 Why should teachers try to make rubrics more rigorous to challenge students to excel?

5 Why should teams work together to create common rubrics to target power standards?

Action Steps

List three action steps you plan to take to include more rigorous rubrics in your assessment repertoire.

Step 1:

Step 2:

Step 3:

7

Formative Assessment Tools:
Real Time and Real Fast

Many instructional strategies also serve as formative assessments. They provide immediate feedback to teachers so that they can adjust their instruction and quickly implement appropriate interventions to clarify misunderstandings before students score poorly on summative assessments and final evaluations.

What Is the New Model of Formative Assessment?

Formative assessments provide specific standards-based feedback that leads to improved student achievement. By using a variety of assessment tools to monitor students' progress toward meeting curriculum goals and state standards, teachers assess where students are and then make effective and immediate decisions about what to do next to help struggling learners and to challenge accelerated learners.

According to Hoover (2009, p. 24), the assessment of struggling learners used to focus on "attempting to identify potential 'deficits' within the learner while simultaneously assuming that lack of progress toward academic or social-emotional benchmarks or objectives was predominately due to something going on 'within' the learner." Under this "deficit assessment model," students could go on for "two or three years struggling in learning before concentrated attention was paid to their needs" (Hoover, 2009, p. 25). Today, however, under the response to intervention (RTI) model, there is "an emphasis on proper instruction first," along with "frequent assessments or *progress monitoring*" (p. 25) to ensure timely interventions.

Since formative assessment provides ongoing monitoring of student progress, it correlates with this shift in emphasis. Teachers have the flexibility to change strategies immediately rather than waiting until the summative assessment, when it is often too late to help the student. Instead of looking for deficits in students who struggle academically or socially, teachers and districts now take responsibility for identifying and meeting those students' needs. A famous cartoon shows a master trying to teach his dog a new trick. The dog fails miserably, and the owner says, "I said I taught him—I didn't say he learned it!" Some teachers are similarly defensive: "I covered the material, but they didn't get it!" The new response to that statement could be, "Well, what did you try next?" The philosophy that "failure is not an option" is a paradigm shift for many educators (Blankstein, 2004).

The emphasis on continuous assessment challenges those teachers who prefer teaching from Monday through Thursday and testing on Friday. They administer quizzes or tests to see what their students learned or did not learn throughout the week. These formal assessments do not allow many do-overs if students score poorly. Moreover, because of the amount of curriculum and standards that must be covered, teachers feel obligated to move on to the next unit, regardless of whether or not all students have achieved understanding.

In contrast, Shores (2009) recommends using both formal and informal formative assessments to check for understanding *daily* so that teachers can quickly adjust instruction and provide additional interventions as needed. Since criterion-based checklists and rubrics assess more open-ended and time-consuming projects and performances, they could be classified as more formal formative assessments. They require a great deal of time and effort to create and implement, and they are often designed by teams of teachers as common assessments. In addition to these more formal and standards-aligned formative assessments, teachers need some quick and effective informal assessment tools that will blend seamlessly into instruction and provide immediate feedback about how students are doing. These tools also serve as instructional strategies, but one should never be able to tell when instruction ends and assessment begins, since the process should be one continuous loop of teach-test-reflect-reteach (if needed)-test again (if needed)-reflect.

What Are Some Informal Formative Assessment Tools?

There are a myriad of shorter, more informal formative assessment tools that can be woven seamlessly throughout instruction. In fact, effective teachers continuously integrate assessment and instruction because they identify a learning problem a student is having and switch to another teaching or assessing strategy almost immediately. The act of *processing information* is difficult for many students. Many informal formative assessment tools, therefore, involve asking students to reflect on what they have learned. Teachers use interpersonal activities that provide insights into areas that need more clarification. The following quick and easy assessment tools encourage active learning. The key is to develop an ever-expanding arsenal of these tools because a particular strategy may be exciting the first time it is introduced, but three weeks of journal writing in middle school, for example, will get old quickly for students. Implementing a variety of processing and reflective strategies energizes both teachers and students.

Sticky Note Exit Poster

The sticky note exit poster strategy allows students to convey their feelings in a private manner. As students leave the room, they place a sticky note on a poster near the door. The sticky note might contain a comment, a question, a concern, a correction to what the teacher said, or a suggestion to address related topics of interest. Visual and kinesthetic learners love sticky notes because they come in multiple sizes and colors. Teachers could have a collection of notes in various colors and different sizes, as well as some that are ruled for the more linear students. Students who have "short and sweet" comments will know to select a small sticky note, whereas students who write big or have more to say might need a larger note. The colors could be designated as well. Yellow notes (the most common) could be used for more general comments, blue notes could be used for what students learned, and neon pink or neon green could be used for big questions that must be addressed the next day. This quick assessment at the end of a class or day not only provides valuable feedback to the teacher but also motivates the visual, kinesthetic, intrapersonal, and verbal/linguistic learners. If students arrange their sticky notes by color or size in neat categories, the more logical learners will activate their logical/mathematical intelligence. Teachers can begin the next day's class by referring to the sticky notes, reviewing what was learned, clarifying any concerns, and answering any questions before moving on to the next lesson.

Top-Ten List

Talk-show host David Letterman popularized the "Top-Ten List," which takes a topic, describes ten details related to it, and ranks them in descending order from ten to one. Some of the items in the list are ridiculous, but most have just enough factual information to be plausible. To turn this game into a classroom activity, teachers could post a topic or question on the board to start the discussion, and students could volunteer items until the whole class has generated its own top-ten list. Topics could include:

- Top Ten Challenges Facing the President
- Top Ten Reasons Students Love Math
- Top Ten Facts to Justify Awarding _____ a Pulitzer Prize for Literature
- Top Ten Challenges from Global Warming

By the time the entire class has arrived at the number-one reason, fact, or challenge, the students have heard nine other ideas that may be factual or funny. This activity fosters creativity, a sense of humor, and, for younger students, the ability to count backward from ten to one (logical/mathematical activity). It is also an innovative way to summarize a lesson and achieve closure on the class or day.

The Human Rubric

Another kinesthetic and interpersonal strategy to help students process information is the "human rubric." To begin this activity, teachers ask the entire class a question that lends itself to ranked responses. Then they post signs displaying scores from 1 to 4 (the usual arrangement of rubrics) about five feet apart on a wall. Each sign can also include a key phrase—a rating, a feeling, or an opinion, depending on the question—that corresponds to the score. Students form their human rubric by lining up under the sign on the wall that best matches their personal response to the question. Figure 7.1 (page 122) offers some examples of questions and ranked responses that could be used in the human rubric.

How would you rate your ability to meet the standard?			
1 Novice (Not yet)	2 In Progress (I am trying!)	3 Meets Standard (I did it!)	4 Exceeds Standard (I'm awesome!)
How do you feel about _____ **(controversial statement)?**			
1 Strongly Disagree or Don't Really Care!	2 Not Sure!	3 I Agree!	4 I Strongly Agree!
How valuable was this information for you?			
1 Will never, ever need it or use it—ever!	2 Could be useful sometime—some- where!	3 Will help me in school, career, or life!	4 Will help me succeed in all I do for the rest of my life!

Figure 7.1: Possible questions for human rubrics.

Teachers could first ask a few volunteers to line up under the number/phrase that best describes their feelings and explain to the class why they chose it. Later, the rest of the class would do the same. The human rubric, much like its twin the human graph (Bellanca & Fogarty, 2003), allows teachers to find out where students are having difficulties and to ascertain students' perceptions about what they are learning. The feedback from the human rubric also lets students know they are not alone when it comes to their feelings.

The human rubric can be used as a preassessment at the beginning of a unit to determine students' prior knowledge and initial feelings. It can be used in the middle of a unit to measure progress, and again at the end of a unit to see how understanding and feelings have changed. During the unit, teachers ask questions to find out why students seem to be having problems. At the end of the unit, they should try to find out what students did, heard, saw, or learned during instruction that caused them to stand under the rating that reflects their final opinion. Rubrics reinforce the criterion-referenced approach to quality teaching and learning, and the human rubric adds an interactive element to formative assessment.

How Can Logs Be Used for Formative Assessment?

Belgrad, Burke, and Fogarty (2008) recommend that teachers introduce students early in the year to authentic assessment tools that will engage them in metacognitive processes. They believe that "by providing guided practice in the [use] of learning logs and pictorial lists, checklists, and scoring rubrics across all subject areas, teachers can ensure that students will become accurate and reflective participants in their own learning and assessment" (p. 134).

Logs are graphic organizers that allow students to keep their own records of what they are learning. They usually consist of short, objective entries that could be about problem solving, reading, vocabulary terms, mathematics symbols, or key ideas from a lecture, video, or experiment (Burke, 2009). Logs help students process information and reflect on their learning. They are a quick and easy assessment tool, providing feedback to students and their teachers about what the students know and need to find out. Teachers use logs as checkpoints to assess students' understanding and respond with additional or more intensive interventions for students who are struggling.

A variety of formats are suitable for learning logs. Logs that are arranged in a grid format give teachers considerable flexibility. They can be assigned to individual students as homework, or they can be introduced as a group activity in which teams of students collaborate to fill them in. Teachers can use grid logs to differentiate instruction by filling in varying amounts of information before students start working on them. The logs for struggling students have fewer blank boxes than those for high-ability students.

The "water cycle vocabulary log" in figure 7.2 is an example of a grid log used with fourth-grade students who are studying a science unit that addresses the standard "Students will differentiate between states of water and how they relate to the water cycle." Teachers have listed the key vocabulary words from the standard in the first column and then left blank boxes for students to fill in under the categories of "definition," "example," and "where the information was found." One row has been completely filled in to show students how to complete the log. A method to differentiate this assignment would be to provide a word bank or to fill in more of the boxes. Students who struggle with written communication could demonstrate their understanding of the material by drawing pictures or telling the teacher the answers orally.

Word	Definition	Example	Where the Information Was Found
Solid	Matter that retains its shape and density when not confined	Ice	Science textbook and the Internet
Liquid			
Gas			
Precipitation			
Condensation			
Freezing point of water			
Boiling point of water			

Created by Carrie Bette-Duncan, Scherry Lewis, Barbara Michalove, Halley Page, and Claire Smith; Clarke County School District; Athens, Georgia. Used with permission.

Figure 7.2: Water cycle vocabulary log for grade-4 science unit.

Figure 7.3 is a science vocabulary log designed by a team of teachers for fifth-grade students who are studying the differences between physical and chemical changes. The teachers have already filled in one definition and one example and provided one picture. The addition of a column for illustrations taps students' visual intelligence. Students may draw original work, use clip art from the computer, or cut out pictures. The vocabulary log is a motivating formative assessment that makes studying standards-based words more interesting and interactive than taking traditional vocabulary quizzes.

Word	Definition	Example	Illustration
Physical change			
Mixture	Two items can be put together and taken back apart		
Separate			
Temperature			
Chemical change		Making oobleck	
Solution			

Created by Jan Miller-Burkins, Karen Higginbotham, Bertha Troutman-Rambeau, and Hallie Williamson; Clarke County School District; Athens, Georgia. Used with permission.

Figure 7.3: Grade-5 science vocabulary log.

Logs provide an efficient formative assessment tool to ascertain what students know or don't know, as well as who knows what and who still needs to know something. In other words, based on the information gathered, teachers can reteach basic terms to the whole class, a small group of students, or just one student. Logs can also be used as summative assessments at the end of a unit to see what students have learned, and many teachers include the log grid in their final tests. They usually vary the blanks or add new terms to extend students' learning beyond rote memorization.

Figure 7.4 shows a completed mathematics vocabulary log for a third-grade unit on measurement. Students could have spent several lessons, days, or weeks working to complete the log by starting with the measurement term, labeling it as being either standard or metric, giving a description or an example of the term, giving equivalents, and listing two things that can be measured using the unit of measurement. The completed log can serve as a graphic organizer and study guide to help all students learn the differences between the measurement terms.

Measurement Term	Standard or Metric?	Description or Example	Equivalents	2–3 Things Measured Using This Unit
Inch	Standard	The last joint of one's thumb Small paper clip	12 in a foot 36 in a yard 2.54 centimeters	Photographs Paper Height
Foot	Standard	A grown man's shoe Distance from elbow to end of pinky	12 inches in a foot 3 in a yard 5,280 in a mile	Height Boards (lumber)
Yard	Standard	A kid's giant step Height of a desk	1,760 in a mile 3 feet 36 inches	Football field Swimming pool Fabric
Mile	Standard	Walk in 20 minutes 20 laps in the gym 4 laps on the field/track	1,760 yards 5,280 feet 63,360 inches	Distance between cities Distances between places in a city
Millimeter	Metric	Thickness of a fingernail Thickness of an eyelash	10 in a centimeter 1,000 in a meter	Hex bolts Spark plug gaps
Centimeter	Metric	Width of front tooth Width of pinky nail	100 in a meter 10,000 in a kilometer	Height Paper

Figure 7.4: Completed grade-3 mathematics vocabulary log for units of measurement.

continued on next page →

Measurement Term	Standard or Metric?	Description or Example	Equivalents	2–3 Things Measured Using This Unit
Meter	Metric	Height of half cabinets Width of 2 student desks Length of long chart paper	1,000 in a kilometer 100 centimeters	Foot races Swimming races
Kilometer	Metric	3 kilometers in 5 miles	1,000 meters	Distance between places Road races (5K, 10K)

Created by Kate Arnold, Daphne Hall, Lisa Lane, and Lisa Stanzi; Clarke County School District; Athens, Georgia. Used with permission.

Once students have studied the material in the completed log, teachers can remove some answers and ask students to fill in the blanks. Figure 7.5 is a version of the log that can be used as a formative assessment while students are still in the process of learning the material. The teacher can leave additional blanks to challenge proficient students or provide a word bank or fill in more boxes to mediate instruction for struggling students. If this informal assessment reveals that the whole class is having difficulty understanding particular concepts, the teacher can reteach specific measurement terms. Students can be assigned to flexible groups to work on the terms based on their levels, or the teacher can work one-on-one with a student who is having difficulty with one or more areas of the material. The teacher can also ask a paraprofessional or special education teacher to help a student work on specific skill areas rather than on the broad standard.

This same informal assessment could be modified to become the final summative assessment when the unit ends and students must demonstrate their understanding of units of measurement one last time. Recall that a formative assessment converts to a summative assessment when the purpose of administering it is to make a final judgment, evaluate whether or not the student has met the standard, or determine the final grade for the unit.

Measurement Term	Standard or Metric?	Description or Example	Equivalents	2–3 Things Measured Using This Unit
Inch	_____	The last joint of one's thumb Small paper clip	____ in a foot 36 in a yard 2.54 centimeters	_____ _____ _____

Figure 7.5: Partially completed grade-3 mathematics vocabulary log for formative assessment.

Measurement Term	Standard or Metric?	Description or Example	Equivalents	2–3 Things Measured Using This Unit
Foot	_____	A grown man's shoe Distance from elbow to end of pinky	12 inches in a foot _____ in a yard 5,280 in a mile	_____
Yard	_____	A kid's giant step Height of a desk	_____ feet _____ inches	_____ _____
Mile	_____	Walk in 20 minutes 4 laps on the field/track	1,760 yards 5,280 feet 63,360 inches	_____
Millimeter	_____	Thickness of ___ _____	10 in a centimeter _____ in a meter	Hex bolts Spark plug gaps
Centimeter	_____	Width of front tooth Width of pinky nail	100 in a meter 10,000 in a kilometer	Height Paper
Meter	_____	_____	1,000 in a kilometer 100 centimeters	Foot races _____
Kilometer	_____	3 kilometers in 5 miles	_____ meters	Distance between places Road races (5K, 10K)

Created by Kate Arnold, Daphne Hall, Lisa Lane, and Lisa Stanzi; Clarke County School District; Athens, Georgia. Used with permission.

Figure 7.6 gives examples of partial grid logs from other subject areas. The examples show the kinds of categories that teachers might use and provide one answer for each category. Note that grid logs can be constructed to assess concepts as well as vocabulary.

Reading/Literature		
Author	**Major Work**	**One Famous Character in Work**
Mark Twain	*Huckleberry Finn*	Tom Sawyer
Writing/Literature		
Literary Term	**Definition**	**Example**
Theme	The message or moral of the work	Man's inhumanity to man
Social Studies		
Leader	**Country**	**Known for**
Stalin	Russia	Leader in WWII, invading Germany, purges
Art		
Term	**Definition**	**Where Will You Find One?**
Mosaic	The process of making pictures or designs by inlaying small bits of colored stone, glass, tile, and so on, in mortar	St. Peter's Basilica in Rome
Music		
Term	**Definition**	**Opposite**
Soprano	The highest singing voice, usually ranging two octaves or more up from the middle; the voice or singer with such a range	Bass

Figure 7.6: Partial logs for six content areas.

Geometry		
Shape	**Draw It**	**Characteristics**
Triangle	△	3 equal lines

What Are Some Other Graphic Organizers to Use for Formative Assessments?

As seen in the previous section on learning logs, teachers can use graphic organizers as instructional tools for introducing information. They can also use them as formative assessments to provide feedback and practice for students. Finally, they can use them as summative evaluations at the end of units to assess student learning.

Agree/Disagree Charts

It is helpful for teachers to find out what students know or think they know about a topic *before* a unit begins. The agree/disagree chart (Bellanca, 2007) is a graphic organizer that can be used for this purpose. The left-hand column of the chart lists six to ten statements about a topic. Some of the statements could be true, some of the statements could be false, and some statements could be partially true or deliberately ambiguous. Before the class studies the topic, individuals or groups of students write their initials in either the "agree" or "disagree" column of the "Before Unit" section. Students should be encouraged to discuss why they think the way they do so that teachers can ascertain students' prior knowledge as well as observe which students have a better understanding of the concepts and which students have misconceptions.

Figure 7.7 (page 130) is an agree/disagree chart for a fifth-grade science unit on physical and chemical change. Figure 7.8 (page 131) is an agree/disagree chart for a fourth-grade science unit on the water cycle.

After the topic has been taught, students revisit the chart and write their initials in either the "agree" or "disagree" column of the "After Unit" section. Students who have changed their opinions should explain whether they did so because of new information or because of a different understanding of the concept. The whole class should discuss which specific facts, statistics, or opinions led students to vote the way they did. Students could also write their thoughts in a reflective journal, write a letter or persuasive essay defending their views, or engage in a role play or debate arguing their positions. The graphic allows students to see how opinions can and should change based on current and factual information.

Statement	Before Unit		After Unit	
	Agree	Disagree	Agree	Disagree
1 Striking a match is an example of a physical change.				
2 A physical change is when I outgrow my shoes.				
3 A chemical change happens when I make a fruit salad.				
4 A chemical change happens when I make a fruit smoothie.				
5 I make a physical change when I give someone 4 quarters for a dollar.				
6 I can undo a physical change.				
7 Making oobleck is an example of a chemical change.				
8 Chemical and physical changes are more similar than they are different.				
9 Changing temperature has nothing to do with physical change.				
10 A chemical change changes the mass of a substance.				

Created by Jan Miller-Burkins, Karen Higginbotham, Bertha Troutman-Rambeau, and Hallie Williamson; Clarke County School District; Athens, Georgia. Used with permission.

Figure 7.7: Grade-5 agree/disagree chart for unit on physical and chemical change.

Another way to use the agree/disagree chart is to ask groups of students to generate their own items about a topic. Before the unit begins, students skim the textbook, watch a video, or use the Internet to find information to help them write true, false, or partially true statements related to the topic. Teachers can also wait until the end of the unit and ask students to create an original agree/disagree chart, based on their thorough understanding of the topic, for next semester's or next year's students. The students can be very creative, and their final product can be assessed once they justify all their answers appropriately. Figure 7.9 (page 132) is a template students could use to create their own charts.

Statement	Before Unit		After Unit	
	Agree	Disagree	Agree	Disagree
1 Clouds are made of cotton candy.				
2 Water has to be in a container for you to pick it up.				
3 The water we drink now is the same water the early settlers drank when they arrived in America.				
4 Condensation on a glass of ice water comes from the inside of the glass.				
5 Water can be a solid, a liquid, or a gas.				
6 Rain is the only form of precipitation.				

Created by Carrie Bette-Duncan, Scherry Lewis, Barbara Michalove, Halley Page, and Claire Smith; Clarke County School District; Athens, Georgia. Used with permission.

Figure 7.8: Grade-4 agree/disagree chart for unit on water cycle.

Venn Diagrams

The Venn diagram is another graphic organizer that can be used both as an instructional strategy and as an assessment strategy. The thinking skill of comparing and contrasting requires one to analyze attributes to determine the similarities and differences between two items. The Venn diagram uses intersecting circles to chart what two different things have in common (placed in the middle section, where the circles overlap) and what is unique to each (placed in the non-overlapping sections of the circles). A teacher might introduce a lesson by using the Venn diagram to demonstrate the similarities and differences between two items, but the same Venn could be used later to assess whether students are able to compare and contrast the same items or different items.

Figure 7.10 (page 133) is a Venn diagram that fifth-grade science students might be asked to create to show the similarities and differences between physical and chemical changes. To help students get started, teachers could provide the characteristics for either physical or chemical change and then ask students to fill in the parallel characteristics on the other side of the diagram. They could also provide the characteristics on both sides of the diagram and require students to fill in the similarities in the middle section. To differentiate this assignment for struggling readers or students who require additional interventions, teachers could provide a word bank of key science terms. For students who need a greater challenge, teachers could integrate writing skills into the task and require that the diagram be accompanied by a written comparison/contrast paragraph that synthesizes all the information.

Directions to Students: Write statements about your topic that your research shows are either true, false, or partially true. Distribute the agree/disagree chart to your classmates prior to learning about the topic in class.

Topic: _____

Statement	Before Unit		After Unit	
	Agree	Disagree	Agree	Disagree
1				
2				
3				
4				
5				
6				
7				
8				
9				
10				

Source: Bellanca, J. (2007). *A guide to graphic organizers: Helping students organize and process content for deeper learning* (2nd ed.), p. 107. Thousand Oaks, CA: Corwin Press. Reprinted by permission.

Figure 7.9: Template for student-generated agree/disagree chart.

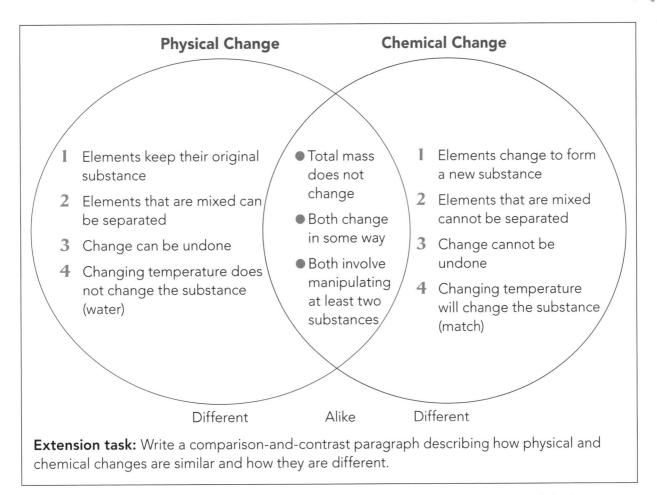

Physical Change

1 Elements keep their original substance
2 Elements that are mixed can be separated
3 Change can be undone
4 Changing temperature does not change the substance (water)

Chemical Change

1 Elements change to form a new substance
2 Elements that are mixed cannot be separated
3 Change cannot be undone
4 Changing temperature will change the substance (match)

- Total mass does not change
- Both change in some way
- Both involve manipulating at least two substances

Different   Alike   Different

Extension task: Write a comparison-and-contrast paragraph describing how physical and chemical changes are similar and how they are different.

Created by Jan Miller-Burkins, Karen Higginbotham, Bertha Troutman-Rambeau, and Hallie Williamson; Clarke County School District; Athens, Georgia. Used with permission.

Figure 7.10: Grade-5 Venn diagram comparing physical change and chemical change.

Figure 7.11 (page 134) shows how teachers can convert the instructive Venn diagram into a formative assessment. Students will receive one point for every correct similarity they write in the middle section of the diagram, as well as one point for every correct difference they identify, as long as the statements of differences on both sides are parallel. The students can also receive ten points for writing the comparison/contrast paragraph that requires them to convey their knowledge of the content in a written format.

How Does Metacognition Support Assessment?

Costa (2008) tells us that the human species is known as "Homo sapiens sapiens," which means a "being that knows its knowing." He says that what distinguishes humans is their ability to stand back and examine their thoughts while engaging in them. This capacity is called "metacognition," or "thinking about our own thinking." Costa says that "although the human brain is capable of generating this reflective consciousness, generally we are not very aware of how we are thinking" (2008, p. 23).

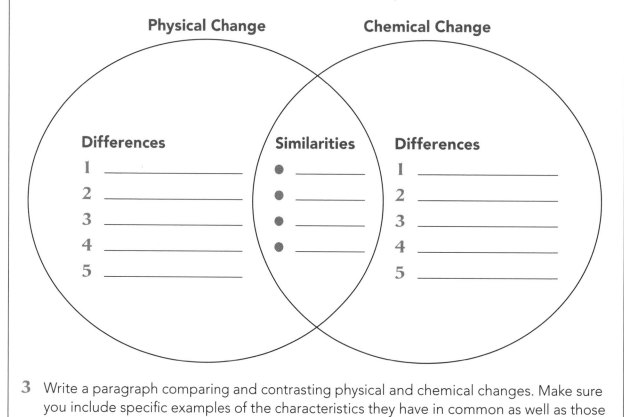

Physical and Chemical Changes Quiz

Directions:

1   You will receive *one point* for every correct statement you write to show how physical and chemical changes are alike (middle section).

2   You will receive *one point* for every correct difference between physical and chemical changes in the outside circles. The statements must be *parallel*.

Physical Change   **Chemical Change**

Differences   **Similarities**   **Differences**

1 _____   • _____   1 _____

2 _____   • _____   2 _____

3 _____   • _____   3 _____

4 _____   • _____   4 _____

5 _____   5 _____

3   Write a paragraph comparing and contrasting physical and chemical changes. Make sure you include specific examples of the characteristics they have in common as well as those that are different (10 points).

Figure 7.11: Venn diagram graphic organizer quiz.

Because there is simply too much content to cover in the limited time teachers have with students, it is essential that teachers prepare students to learn independently and continuously. The key is helping students make judgments about what they learn and about how to apply that knowledge appropriately. Hersh (2009, p. 52) says that teachers must teach students "to think horizontally, crossing disciplines and connecting the dots to make sense of the seemingly infinite information available through information technology and media." Teachers must also help students learn how to reflect on their own work and improve it. Many students are not able to engage in self-reflection or carry on a mental dialogue that poses thoughtful questions. Teachers can give students a feel for these skills by providing them with a series of questions, such as those listed in figure 7.12 (page 136), to help them assess their own products and performances, their group efforts, and their problem-solving skills. Students can respond to the questions either orally or in writing. The scaffolding the teacher provides starts the metacognitive process, but the hope is that students will be able to internalize it. The goal is to help all students become their own "metacognitive monitors" as they master the lifelong dispositions of self-reflection and self-assessment.

Metacognition is critical to both formative and summative assessment. Students who are working on a rough draft of a research paper review the questions on the checklist and ask themselves, "How am I doing?" "What have I done well?" "What do I need to do next?" Learning does not stop, however, once students turn in their final research paper and receive their summative evaluation. Just because they receive a B on the final paper does not mean they stop reflecting on their work. Granted, some students will look at the grade, ignore any teacher comments, and stuff the paper in their English notebook or throw it in the trash. But lifelong learners who have internalized the ability to reflect on their mistakes and learn from them will take the time to formulate new goals for the next research paper they write. Developing cognitive skills is an important goal for students, but developing meta-cognitive skills may be an even more important goal for lifelong learning.

What Are Some Metacognitive Strategies to Use?

One can never be too rich or too thin or have too many different processing strategies to motivate today's Twitter generation. Students are used to visual entertainment and interactive social networks that keep their attention 24/7. Teachers have to compete for their students' attention by constantly introducing new instructional and assessment strategies to keep them engaged. Students need to learn how to pause from their interactive pursuits and reflect on their learning. They also need to learn how to transfer what they learn in class to other classes and to their own lives beyond school.

Time to Think About Questions

If teachers always ask questions to the entire class and wait for students to respond, the same fast-thinking and fast-talking students tend to raise their hands. Often, students don't respect classroom procedures and just blurt out the answers. Many students need more time to process a question, formulate their answers, raise their hands to get recognized, and then reflect on the quality of their own answers or the answers of others. To meet these students' needs, teachers can ask a question and then require students to take a "thinking moment" to reflect quietly on the question and then write three answers to it. This procedure allows all students time to think about the question and practice formulating an answer. Some students may struggle to write only two answers, while others will generate five or six, depending on their ability levels and degree of understanding. If the teacher required just one answer to the question, many students would select the most obvious (and probably the easiest) answer without really digging deeper to search for multiple answers. To come up with three answers, students have to reflect more deeply. Figure 7.13 (page 137) shows three possible answers that students could give to a question that asks them to think about their own thinking.

Self-Reflective Questions

Products

- Did I follow the directions?

- Have I met all the criteria for quality work?

- How would I improve this product?

- How does this product reflect my creativity and originality?

Performances

- How did I meet or exceed the standards?

- How could I make improvements based on my first practice?

- What could I do to keep people's attention?

- How did I "think outside the box" and allow my personality to show?

Group Work

- Do I need to revisit my role assignment?

- How can I contribute more to my group?

- What could I do to encourage group members more?

- How will collaboration help me in the marketplace?

- Why do people label "working cooperatively with others" as a soft skill?

Problem-Solving Skills

- Have I solved a problem like this before?

- Can I break this problem down into parts? How?

- What resources do I need to solve the problem?

- How can I look at this problem in another way?

- What is the real problem?

- Do I possess the resilience to overcome setbacks?

Figure 7.12: Questions to help students develop metacognitive skills.

How do checklists help you think better?

1   Checklists help me get organized and show me what to do next. I need the sequence to guide my thinking.

2   I like the "chunks" in checklists because I can think about one section at a time and not get overwhelmed thinking about the whole assignment. I feel good when I finish each chunk.

3   I like to work with a buddy because he checks my thinking to make sure I understand what I am doing.

● 2 minutes to think

● 3 minutes to write

● 1 minute to share

Figure 7.13: Possible student responses to metacognitive question.

The thinking moment strategy encourages teachers to "ask a good question," to allow time for thinking, to clarify students' thinking, to check for understanding, and to help students whose answers indicate they may be confused.

Text Message/Tweet

Today's social networks encourage communication among friends, but they also require students to be succinct. The thinking skills of summarizing and problem solving are activated when students send text messages or tweets. Teachers can tap into what students do outside of class and use similar formats in class to take a quick read of where students are and what they still need. When a checkpoint arrives and teachers want fast formative feedback or reflection about what students have learned, how they feel about their work, and any questions they still have, the students can respond by simulating text messages and tweets on paper, using the forms shown in figure 7.14 (page 138). Veteran teachers may not be as familiar with today's instant communication etiquette, but they can allude to the telegrams or mailgrams of earlier times, when people paid by the letter or word, thus encouraging everyone to keep it short!

Wraparound Strategy

Even though teachers are usually exhausted at the end of a class period, day, week, or unit (or all of the above), the research suggests that the closure of a lesson is as important as the hook used to get students' attention at the beginning of a lesson. People tend to remember the last things they see, hear, and do, so it is important to reinforce the day's learning. The sticky note exit poster, discussed

Text Message

Date: _____

To (teacher): _____

From (student): _____

Topic: _____

Message: _____

_____

_____

Tweet

Tweet topic: _____

Teacher to whom you are sending the tweet: _____

Your tweet (short message or update of 140 or fewer characters):

_____

_____

Teacher's return tweet:

_____

_____

Send the teacher a nudge if you don't get a response: _____

Figure 7.14: Text message and tweet.

earlier, requires students to write reflections, questions, or concerns before they leave for the day. The wraparound is another metacognitive closure strategy, but it requires students to communicate orally. Teachers begin by posting one or more stems and then ask students to complete a stem. They can ask for volunteers to complete the stem, or they can go around the room (wraparound) and ask each student to respond. Students are allowed to repeat something that someone else said (reinforcement), and they are allowed to pass if they choose. Another strategy is to divide the class into groups (or by rows of seats) and assign one stem to each group or row so that students respond to different stems. They can answer individually or consult their group and share one group response that represents their collective thinking. The wraparound strategy helps individual students focus on at least one statement, but it also gives everyone the opportunity to hear a variety of ideas and reflections on their learnings. Figure 7.15 provides an assortment of wraparound stems that can lead all students to pause, reflect, share, and reflect again to internalize their key ideas before leaving the class or going home at the end of the day.

One idea I learned today is . . .

One thing I am still confused about is . . . because . . .

This topic reminds me of something we studied in another class . . . because . . .

One thing that surprised me is . . . because . . .

I can use this information in my job . . . because . . .

One thing I will remember five years from now is . . . because . . .

One idea I would like to learn more about is . . . because . . .

Today's lesson helped me understand the standard . . . because . . .

Figure 7.15: Wraparound stems for final reflection.

Final Thoughts

Wiliam (2007, p. 191) has argued that

> the kinds of formative assessment practices that profoundly impact student achievement cannot wait until the end of a marking period, or even to the end of an instructional unit. If students have left the classroom before teachers have made adjustments to their teaching on the basis of what they have learned about the students' achievement, then they are already playing catch-up.

Leahy, Lyon, Thompson, and Wiliam (2005) believe that the most important formative assessments are those that occur "minute by minute" and "day by day." The quick informal assessments discussed in this chapter serve as checkpoints between the more rigorous formal assessments. Teachers provide feedback to students in real time and real fast. Many of these quick interactive assessments are not graded; their value is in the immediate feedback they give to teachers so that they can adjust instruction to better meet their students' needs. No student is left to languish for weeks, months, or years without receiving the necessary interventions, as occurred with the "deficit assessment model" mentioned earlier.

Students today want everything fast—food, video games, text messaging, money, and movies on demand. They also want to have their work assessed quickly so they won't get behind and have to play catch-up for the rest of the year. A television commercial for an insurance company uses the slogan "Life comes at you fast." Welcome to the twenty-first century, where both life and assessment come at you fast. The traditional model of teaching from Monday to Thursday and testing on Friday is evolving into the more contemporary model of seamlessly integrating instruction and assessment. Teachers who frequently test students and return the results in a week don't improve learning as much as teachers who give quick and targeted feedback every minute of every day.

Teachers must be flexible in pacing their instruction to allow time to intervene with students who need extra help and to provide enrichment to students who have mastered the learning. As Guskey (2007/2008) notes, "Teachers must keep in mind what the class needs to accomplish by the end of any learning sequence, but they also must see students' pathways to that end in more flexible and accommodating terms" (p. 34). The value of the quick and easy strategies presented in this chapter can be maximized when teachers follow up with the appropriate instructional interventions to correct problems *before* students get left behind.

Concluding Exercises

Reflections on Formative Assessment Tools

1 How are instructional strategies different from formative assessments?

2 Why can vocabulary logs motivate students to study standards-based terminology?

3 How can graphic organizers such as the agree/disagree chart and Venn diagrams make abstract thinking more concrete?

4 Why should teachers build in more class time for students to reflect on their learning?

5 How can informal formative assessments provide valuable feedback in real time to both teachers and students?

Action Steps

List three action steps you plan to take to include more quick formative assessments in your instruction:

Step 1:

Step 2:

Step 3:

8

Summative Assessment and Evaluation: The Last Judgment

The purpose of summative assessment is to provide the *last* opportunity for students to demonstrate their ability to meet standards within a specified learning period. After this final assessment has been administered, teachers synthesize all the formative and summative assessment data they have collected, evaluate the students' work using school or district guidelines, and assign a final grade based upon students' mastery of learning goals.

When Should We Use Summative Assessments?

Summative assessments represent the culminating experience of a learning segment. A learning segment could be a chapter in the textbook, a curriculum unit, the first half of a grading period, an entire course, a quarter, a trimester, a semester, or a year. Summative assessments are usually administered after students have had multiple opportunities to master a skill through instructional guidance, repeated practice, and formative assessments. Airasian (2000, p. 95) says that summative assessments are used to "evaluate, or sum up, the outcomes of instruction." The major difference between formative assessments and summative assessments is their relation to grades. Formative assessments provide feedback and are either not graded or graded but weighted less than summative assessments, since students are still in the "formative stages" of learning. They affect the instructional decisions teachers make during the learning segment. In contrast, summative assessments are almost always graded because their purpose is to determine whether or not the student has mastered the standards, and they are administered at the end of the learning segment. The grade could be in the form of a letter grade, percentage score, or label such as "meets standards" or "exceeds standards." These grades are what Airasian (2000, p. 95) describes as "official grades," because they become part of the students' report cards and permanent records.

What Should Be Graded?

Teachers need to administer summative assessments in order to *prove* students have met curriculum outcomes and learning standards. Most people think of unit tests, end-of-chapter tests, research papers, major presentations, projects, portfolios, midterm examinations, or final examinations as the most obvious examples of summative assessments that are graded. O'Connor (2009, p. 131) recommends that teachers use a combination of assessment types, such as the following, to showcase each student's abilities:

- Paper-and-pencil tests—Primarily for knowledge

- Performance assessments—Primarily for application of knowledge and to recognize skills and behaviors

- Personal communication—To evaluate aspects of all types of learning goals

He compares the process of administering a variety of summative assessments to what license bureaus do to grant driver's licenses:

> First, the driver must usually take a written test on the rules of the road and common driving situations. This is often followed by an eye test, and finally, a performance assessment of the critical skill—driving. Student drivers must pass all three tests to obtain a license. This model can be applied in the classroom when we want students to demonstrate their knowledge, skills, and behaviors. (p. 131)

Of course, students practice their driving skills as they prepare for the driving test at the license bureau, and they receive feedback throughout the formative practice period. By using more than one assessment method, the driving teacher collects sufficient evidence to make a summative judgment about whether the student is competent to drive on public streets. When teachers collect and interpret multiple types of information, they are better able to make key decisions about the student's ability to meet specific goals (curriculum focused, standards based, or safety related).

As mentioned in earlier chapters, a performance assessment such as a research paper can be classified as formative in the initial draft stages, while students are practicing their writing craft, but then classified as summative when the final paper is submitted. Some educators believe in assigning a grade on the basis of the final paper only. They don't record any of the formative assessments (research review, notes, outline, rough drafts, references, editing) that constitute the research process. O'Connor (2007a, p. 138) believes that "teachers should provide feedback on formative assessments (those assessments for learning such as drafts, quizzes, and practice), but determine grades only from the evidence from varied summative assessments (assessments of learning). If we do this, we make grading supportive of learning." O'Connor places homework in the formative category and argues that it should be used to provide feedback and should not be graded. The exception is "homework that requires students to extend or integrate the knowledge, understanding, and skills they have obtained in classroom learning activities—assignments or projects through which students demonstrate application and synthesis of what they have learned in class" (p. 138).

Some districts require teachers to record a certain number of official academic grades throughout a marking period. Many times, teachers have to provide "in progress" grades for midterm report cards and parent conference nights. Since parents want to monitor their children's grades rather than receive a surprise grade at the end of the quarter, they may need daily or weekly feedback. This feedback could be in the form of statements such as "needs additional help," "making progress," or "meets expectations," depending on district guidelines. Teachers might also grade and record some formative assignments but not weigh them as much as the summative assessments at the end of the marking period.

An assignment that addresses only one or two indicators of a standard or a single segment of a curriculum objective may not warrant repeated practice work or a summative assessment. It could be assessed and recorded as a formative assessment during the grading period. Whether students will be allowed to redo the assessment later to earn a higher grade is up to the teacher. Some teachers allow students to redo assignments or retake tests any time before the final grade is submitted. Other teachers set a cutoff date for retakes because they don't want to have students do lackluster work throughout the grading period only to demand retakes on everything the last week. Middle school and high school teachers may work with 150 students at a time, and if all of them wait until the last minute to apply themselves, it might be chaotic. Some teachers worry that students will not take formative assessments seriously if they do not count for something, or that giving the option of retakes may teach students to postpone taking responsibility for their own learning. It is overwhelming when parents demand that their children be allowed to make up missing work or do work over during the last days of a learning segment so that they can earn that A or get the B they need to try out for a sport, stay in the marching band, or get accepted into the National Honor Society.

The entire issue of grading is very controversial and has been covered in depth by Marzano (2006, 2010), Reeves (2004), Guskey (2007/2008), Guskey and Bailey (2001), Chappuis and Chappuis (2007/2008), O'Connor (2007a, 2007b, 2009), and many others. To ensure that all teachers follow appropriate and consistent grading practices, district leaders need to address such issues as assigning zeroes, counting grades at the end of the learning segment more than those at the beginning, grading homework, grading only summative assessments, weighting grades, and dropping grades. Regardless of the guidelines adopted by schools or districts, it is imperative that teachers provide periodic feedback so that all stakeholders are aware of how students are progressing (or not progressing) throughout the marking period.

How Can the Same Assessment Be Used for Both Formative and Summative Purposes?

If teachers create totally different summative assessments for the "last judgment," it seems as if their purpose is to trick students. Everyone remembers an unfair assessment in which teachers asked questions about material that was not covered in the textbook or class discussion or that appeared only in the footnotes of a chapter. Playing "gotcha" with students' lives should not be a purpose of assessment. It is important to challenge students by using different questions or problems to make them think critically rather than just memorizing answers, but the summative assessment should be similar in content and type to the formative assessments that have been used throughout the instructional period. Questions that appeared in earlier homework assignments, quizzes, or tests could appear in a slightly different format on the final exam. Performances such as writing an informational essay could be part of the summative assessment, but without the checklist and rubric that guided students throughout the formative instructional process. Students could be asked to conduct a scientific experiment as part of their final assessment, but without the checklist they used to complete their practice experiments.

Table 8.1 revisits the balanced assessment model from chapter 2, which gives examples of formative assessments (assessments *for* learning) and summative assessments (assessments *of* learning), classified based on their purpose and timing. As explained previously, an assessment is classified as formative when the purpose for using it is to provide constructive and specific feedback early in the learning process. That same assessment is classified as summative when it is used at the end of the learning process for the purpose of making a final judgment on whether or not the student has met the standard.

Table 8.1: The Balanced Assessment Model

Formative Assessment Process Assessment *for* Learning Purpose: Provide ongoing feedback to *improve* learning Timing: During the learning segment	**Summative Assessment Process** Assessment *of* Learning Purpose: Evaluate final efforts to *prove* learning Timing: At the end of the learning segment
Informal teacher questions	Formal oral interview
Conversation with student	Conference with student
Informal observation	Formal observation
Rough drafts of written work	Final copy of written work
Learning log (in progress)	Final learning log entries
Reflective journal (multiple drafts)	Final journal entries
Mathematics problem solving steps	Mathematics final solution
Practice science experiment	Final science experiment
Rehearsal of presentation	Final presentation
Working portfolio	Showcase portfolio
Practice checklist for do-overs	Final checklist
Practice rubrics (analytical)	Final rubrics (analytical or holistic)
Homework, quizzes	Teacher-made tests
Benchmark/interim tests	High-stakes standardized tests

When teacher teams target the standards and create common assessments at the beginning of the learning cycle, they start with the end in mind and then plan backwards to achieve that end. It is not unusual to use a standards-based assessment at the very beginning of the year as a diagnostic tool to determine students' readiness levels. That same assessment could be used as an instructional formative assessment throughout the learning period to help teachers identify students who are struggling. And the same assessment could then be used at the end of the learning cycle as the final summative assessment to determine whether or not the students have met their goals.

Are Benchmark Tests Formative or Summative Assessments?

Many districts and most commercial vendors label benchmark or interim assessments as formative, because they say their purpose is to provide short-cycle feedback to teachers about students' progress toward meeting the standards that will be measured on the high-stakes summative tests. Districts purchase these assessments and have teachers administer them at specified intervals to find out which students are mastering the standards and which students need more help on targeted areas. Huebner (2009, p. 85) points out that, "unlike summative assessments, . . . interim assessments take place in time for teachers to adjust instruction to address any identified gaps in student mastery."

Chappuis and Chappuis (2007/2008) believe that even though the assessments may be intended to guide further instruction for individual students or groups of students, teachers and administrators may not know how to use the results to drive instruction. They may regard benchmark tests simply as "practice summative tests" or checkpoints to gauge students' readiness to pass the high-stakes standardized tests administered toward the end of the school year. Chappuis and Chappuis point out that "the assessments will produce no formative benefits if teachers administer them, report the results, and then continue with instruction as previously planned—as can easily happen when teachers are expected to cover a hefty amount of content in a given time" (2007/2008, p. 16). If, however, teachers take the time to analyze the results and target those areas in which individual students or groups of students scored poorly, they can help students improve their skills and their academic achievement.

What Is Evaluation?

Even though most assessments can be classified as either formative or summative, depending on their purpose and timing, both types of assessment are used to arrive at an *evaluation* of individual students. According to Airasian (2000, p. 10), "evaluation occurs after assessment information has been collected, synthesized, and thought about, because that is when the teacher is in a position to make informed judgments." Butler and McMunn (2006) believe that these judgments should be based on *multiple sources* of assessment information. They explain that teachers should

> envision each formative classroom assessment as a snapshot of what students know and are able to do. A number of these snapshots can be collected into an album and used as evidence in an evaluation. This evaluation process goes beyond just collecting information, however; evaluation is concerned with making judgments about the collection. Evaluation thus involves placing a "value" on the collection. (p. 2)

Teachers who collect a variety of formative "snapshots" that include quizzes, homework, journals, graphic organizers, research papers, projects, and multimedia presentations possess a photo album or academic portfolio that offers a more vivid and accurate portrait of the student as a learner than any one assessment. After teachers collect and analyze *all* the multiple assessments, they evaluate the collection. The evaluation is the final judgment as to whether or not the student has met the standards and achieved the curriculum goals. It can be represented by a letter grade, a percentage grade, or a descriptor such as "needs improvement," "meets standards," "exceeds standards," "pass," or "fail," depending on the grading system used. Nitko (2004, p. 9) notes that the summative evaluation of students means "judging the quality or worth of a student's achievement after the instructional process is completed. Giving letter grades on report cards is one example of reporting your summative evaluation of a student's achievement."

Summative evaluations have a tremendous impact on the lives of students. Grades affect a student's self-esteem and social status among peers. They are also a major (sometimes the only) factor in decisions about academic tracking, promotion, retention, summer school attendance, eligibility for athletics and extracurricular activities, placement on honor rolls, membership in honor societies, financial grants, scholarships, selection of valedictorians and salutatorians, college admissions, and employment opportunities. In many cases, final grades determine a student's future success in school, the marketplace, and life!

As noted earlier, district leaders need to clearly communicate grading and reporting guidelines to ensure consistency and reliability throughout the district. Teachers need to know what grades should be included and how they should be evaluated, weighted, and reported. They need to know whether to use a point system, letter grades, or percentages and whether to eliminate zeroes and lowest grades or add bonus points and extra credit. It is advisable to follow the district guidelines when it comes to grading and reporting issues, but educators should work within the system to propose a more realistic and equitable approach to grading if the current one needs improvement.

Many systems are adopting what Marzano (2010) calls a "standards-referenced" report card that focuses on the major strands of the state standards and provides more specific feedback on key skills. For example, instead of simply giving a student a B in language arts, which represents a composite evaluation of that student's reading, writing, and communication skills, a teacher analytically scores the student on each component of the language arts standards. A student might receive feedback on each of the following skills:

- Reading comprehension
- Reading fluency
- Listening skills
- Speaking skills
- Informational writing
- Narrative writing
- Response to literature
- Writing usage
- Conventions (spelling, punctuation, and capitalization)

The report card also shows an overall grade of some form that summarizes all of the multiple skills.

Districts throughout the United States are struggling to develop more effective grading and reporting systems that will reflect the focus on standards. This process may eventually become the subject of a national debate if national standards are adopted and state standards cease to exist.

Are Standardized Test Scores More Valid Than Teachers' Evaluations?

Even though valid and reliable teacher-made assessments provide the most accurate information for judging a student's academic ability, the value of school grades is often questioned. Unfortunately, some parents, many newspaper reporters, and most politicians assume that the results of external high-stakes standardized tests are more valid and reliable than the evaluation of classroom teachers. Davies (2007, p. 35), however, cites 2006 research from the Assessment Reform Group, which found that "when a teacher's professional judgment regarding the quality of student work is based on knowledge arising from the conscientious development and application of consistent criteria for summative evaluation, the teacher's judgments are likely to be more valid and reliable than the results of external tests." To ensure sound evaluation, Davies notes,

> it is essential that evidence of learning be triangulated (collected from multiple sources and in multiple forms) and collected over time. And when teachers work together and develop clearly specified criteria that describe progressive levels of competence and procedures for using criteria to evaluate student work, they are more able to reliably assess and evaluate a greater range of classroom work. (2007, p. 35)

How Are Programs and Teachers Evaluated?

While we usually think of assessment in relation to tracking and evaluating a student's individual growth, one of the main purposes of assessment is to gather data that can be used to evaluate the effectiveness of a program, an instructional strategy, or a textbook. The final evaluation, based upon multiple data points, will help decision makers determine whether to keep, modify, or eliminate the program, strategy, or textbook for the next year. It won't help this year's students, but it might help next year's students.

Teachers can also self-assess their own effectiveness in implementing a strategy or program. Popham (1999, p. 298) says that "when teachers evaluate their instructional endeavors, they're really evaluating the quality of the instructional program they put together as well as the way they delivered that program." Based on the feedback they obtain from administering formative assessments, teachers make adjustments to improve their implementation. At the end of the year, students' summative assessments reflect a teacher's effectiveness and might be submitted to a supervisor as evidence in the formal teacher evaluation process.

Final Thoughts

The word *summative* seems so final. It has taken on almost sinister connotations: the "last judgment," the "end of the road," or the "last hurrah." Many people equate summative assessments with high-stakes standardized tests that give students one chance to score high enough to get promoted or to graduate. Educators, however, should realize that most summative classroom assessments are natural extensions of formative classroom assessments. A teacher can even use the same test as both a formative assessment and a summative assessment. How it is classified depends on its purpose (to provide feedback or to determine a grade) and its timing (early in the teaching and learning process or at the end).

Even though many teachers prefer not to label or sort students by giving grades, most education systems require that teachers assign grades to summative assessments to signify whether students have met, exceeded, or failed to meet learning goals on specific standards-based tasks. At the end of the designated learning segment, teachers review multiple formative and summative assessments designed in multiple formats. They synthesize and interpret all the data—often putting more emphasis on students' most current work, which reflects the progress they have made—and place a value on the "body of evidence." This evaluation translates into the final grade that appears on the official report card. The entire grading, evaluation, and reporting process is controversial because of all the variables involved, but educational researchers and practitioners around the United States are engaged in an effort to establish criteria that will help standardize the process and make it more transparent to teachers, students, parents, and the public at large.

Concluding Exercises

Reflections on Summative Assessment and Evaluation

1 When should teachers administer summative assessments?

2 What are some of the controversies surrounding grading and reporting?

3 Why are both formative and summative assessments used to arrive at a final evaluation of a student's knowledge and skills?

4 Do you think benchmark or interim assessments should be classified as formative or summative? Explain your reasons.

5 Why can teachers' evaluations of students be more accurate than standardized test scores?

Action Steps

List three action steps you plan to take regarding your summative assessment and evaluation process.

Step 1:

Step 2:

Step 3:

Epilogue

The required educational measurement course that most educators took in their undergraduate certification program does not begin to prepare teachers for today's assessment challenges. Knowing how to compute the mean, the median, and the mode for test scores seems as archaic as using the ditto machine to reproduce worksheets. Assessment drives instruction, and teachers who rely on prepackaged or textbook-driven worksheets, quizzes, or tests will not be able to help their students meet the state standards as measured by high-stakes standardized tests.

Most educators today understand the importance of implementing a variety of assessments in order to measure student progress toward different goals and to arrive at a more accurate appraisal of student achievement. However, Chappuis, Chappuis, and Stiggins (2009, p. 15) warn that "the use of multiple measures does not, by itself, translate into high-quality evidence. Using misinformation to triangulate on student needs defeats the purpose of bringing in more results to inform our decisions." Their answer is to "build balanced assessment systems with assessment-literate users" (p. 19). Huebner (2009, p. 85) agrees that "the challenge for schools is designing a balanced assessment system using the strengths of summative, interim, and formative assessments to address instructional, accountability, and learning needs." This "union of insufficiencies," to use Shulman's (1988) phrase, provides a more complete portrait of the student as a learner than any one type of assessment used in isolation.

Today's teachers assume tremendous responsibility for helping all students succeed and for eliminating the achievement gap that separates black and Latino student performance from white student performance by as many as three or four years. The McKinsey & Company (2009) report *The Economic Impact of the Achievement Gap in America's Schools* found that for many students, "lagging achievement evidenced as early as fourth grade appears to be a powerful predictor" of low high school and college graduation rates, as well as reduced lifetime earnings, adverse health conditions, and low civic engagement (p. 6). Despite the statistics, the report maintains that

> today's achievement gap can be substantially closed. Many teachers and schools across the country are proving that race and poverty are not destiny; many more are demonstrating that middle-class children can be educated to world-class levels of performance. America's history of bringing disadvantaged groups into the economic mainstream over time, and the progress of other nations in education, suggest that large steps forward are possible. (McKinsey & Company, 2009, p. 6)

Teacher teams who develop and use valid and reliable formative and summative common assessments can help close the achievement gap and help all students learn the skills they need to meet and exceed state, national, and international standards.

Assessment is a critical component of the education reform movement that is moving from the No Child Left Behind approach to the "All Children on Track for Success" paradigm. Teachers must challenge the whole child and prepare every student to meet the requirements of the twenty-first century. The intent of this book has been to offer a balance of formative and summative strategies that will support struggling students and motivate and challenge all students. Hopefully the book has also provided the rationale for correlating all assessments to state standards.

Despite the billions of dollars spent on prescriptive instructional and assessment programs, teacher-created assessments provide the most specific and immediate feedback to help students achieve and succeed. When teams of teachers collaborate to create, administer, score, and examine student work, they work as a community of assessors to determine what they need to do in real time to meet the real needs of their diverse students. It takes a village to help a child, and a team of dedicated, assessment-literate, and empowered teachers can make a difference in one child's life as well as the lives of students everywhere. When teachers skillfully balance formative and summative assessments and integrate them seamlessly into their instruction, they improve student learning. Assessment-literate teachers instill confidence in their students. Most importantly, they help them become lifelong learners and productive adults who contribute to society and pass on their love of learning to the next generation.

References

Ainsworth, L. (2007). Common formative assessments: The centerpiece of an integrated standards-based assessment system. In D. Reeves (Ed.), *Ahead of the curve: The power of assessment to transform teaching and learning* (pp. 79–101). Bloomington, IN: Solution Tree Press.

Ainsworth, L., & Viegut, D. (2006). *Common formative assessments: How to connect standards-based instruction and assessment.* Thousand Oaks, CA: Corwin Press.

Airasian, P. W. (2000). *Assessment in the classroom: A concise approach.* Boston: McGraw-Hill.

Ataya, R. L. (2007). Policy and technical considerations for classroom assessment. In P. Jones, J. F. Carr, & R. L. Ataya (Eds.), *A pig don't get fatter the more you weigh it: Classroom assessments that work* (pp. 71–86). New York: Teachers College Press.

Belgrad, S., Burke, K., & Fogarty, R. (2008). *The portfolio connection: Student work linked to standards* (3rd ed.). Thousand Oaks, CA: Corwin Press.

Bellanca, J. (2007). *A guide to graphic organizers: Helping students organize and process content for deeper learning* (2nd ed.). Thousand Oaks, CA: Corwin Press.

Bellanca, J., & Fogarty, R. (2003). *Blueprints for achievement in the cooperative classroom* (3rd ed.). Thousand Oaks, CA: Corwin Press.

Black, P. J., & Wiliam, D. (1998). Inside the black box: Raising standards through classroom assessment. *Phi Delta Kappan, 80*(2), 139–148.

Blankstein, A. M. (2004). *Failure is not an option: Six principles that guide student achievement in high-performing schools.* Thousand Oaks, CA: Corwin Press and the Hope Foundation.

Bloom, B. (Ed.) (1956). *Taxonomy of educational objectives.* New York: Longman.

Blythe, T., Allen, D., & Powell, B. S. (2008). *Looking together at student work* (2nd ed.). New York: Teachers College Press.

Bridgeland, J. M., Dilulio, J. J., Jr., & Morison, K. B. (2006, March). *The silent epidemic: Perspectives of high school dropouts.* Accessed at www.civicenterprises.net/pdfs/thesilentepidemic3-06.pdf on November 12, 2009.

Brookhart, S. M. (2008). *How to give effective feedback to your students.* Alexandria, VA: Association for Supervision and Curriculum Development.

Burke, K. (2006). *From standards to rubrics in six steps: Tools for assessing student learning, K–8.* Thousand Oaks, CA: Corwin Press.

Burke, K. (2009). *How to assess authentic learning* (5th ed.). Thousand Oaks, CA: Corwin Press.

Butler, S. M., & McMunn, N. D. (2006). *A teacher's guide to classroom assessment: Understanding and using assessment to improve student learning.* San Francisco: Jossey-Bass.

Chappuis, S., & Chappuis, J. (2007/2008, December/January). The best value in formative assessment. *Educational Leadership, 65*(4), 14–18.

Chappuis, S., Chappuis, J., & Stiggins, R. (2009). The quest for quality. *Educational Leadership 67*(3), 15–19.

Common Core State Standards Initiative. (2009, October 1). *News release.* Accessed at www.corestandards .org on November 10, 2009.

Costa, A. L. (2008). The thought-filled curriculum. *Educational Leadership, 65*(5), 20–24.

Darling-Hammond, L. (2009). We must strip away layers of inequality. *Journal of Staff Development, 30*(2), 52–56.

Darling-Hammond, L., & McCloskey, L. (2008). Assessment for learning around the world: What would it mean to be internationally competitive? *Phi Delta Kappan, 90*(4), 263–272.

Davies, A. (2007). Involving students in the classroom assessment process. In D. Reeves (Ed.), *Ahead of the curve: The power of assessment to transform teaching and learning* (pp. 31–57). Bloomington, IN: Solution Tree Press.

Drake, S. M., & Burns, R. C. (2004). *Meeting standards through integrated curriculum.* Alexandria, VA: Association for Supervision and Curriculum Development.

Easton, L. B. (2009). Protocols: A facilitator's best friend. *Tools for Schools, 12*(3), 1–2.

Erkens, C. (2009). Developing our assessment literacy. In T. Guskey (Ed.), *The teacher as assessment leader* (pp. 11–30). Bloomington, IN: Solution Tree Press.

Finn, C. E., & Petrilli, M. J. (2009, March 11). Stimulating a race to the top. *Education Week*, p. 31.

Fogarty, R. (2001). *Differentiated learning: Different strokes for different folks.* Thousand Oaks, CA: Corwin Press.

Fuhrman, S. H., Resnick, L., & Shepard, L. (2009, October 14). Standards aren't enough. *Education Week*, p. 28.

Gardner, H. (1993). *Frames of mind: The theory of multiple intelligences* (10th ed.). New York: Basic Books.

Gareis, C. R., & Grant, L. W. (2008). *Teacher-made assessments: How to connect curriculum, instruction, and student learning.* Larchmont, NY: Eye On Education.

Garner, B. K. (2007). *Getting to got it! Helping struggling students learn how to learn.* Alexandria, VA: Association for Supervision and Curriculum Development.

Garner, B. K. (2008). When students seem stalled. *Educational Leadership, 65*(6), 32–38.

Georgia Department of Education. (2010). *Georgia performance standards: English language arts and reading K–5.* Accessed at https://www.georgiastandards.org/Standards/pages/BrowseStandards/ELAStandardsK-5 .aspx on November 11, 2009.

Graseck, S. (2009). Teaching with controversy. *Educational Leadership, 67*(1), 45–49.

Guskey, T. R. (2007). Using assessments to improve teaching *and* learning. In D. Reeves (Ed.), *Ahead of the curve: The power of assessment to transform teaching and learning* (pp. 15–29). Bloomington, IN: Solution Tree Press.

Guskey, T. R. (2007/2008). The rest of the story: The power of formative assessment depends on how you use the results. *Educational Leadership, 65*(4), 28–35.

Guskey, T. R., & Bailey, J. M. (2001). *Developing grading and reporting systems for student learning.* Thousand Oaks, CA: Corwin Press.

Hersh, R. H. (2009). A well-rounded education for a flat world. *Educational Leadership, 67*(1), 51–53.

Hierck, T. (2009). Differentiated pathways to success. In T. Guskey (Ed.), *The teacher as assessment leader* (pp. 249–262). Bloomington, IN: Solution Tree Press.

Hoover, J. J. (2009). *RTI: Assessment essentials for struggling learners.* Thousand Oaks, CA: Corwin Press.

Hord, S. M., & Sommers, W. A. (2008). *Leading professional learning communities: Voices from research and practice.* Thousand Oaks, CA: Corwin Press and National Association of Secondary School Principals.

Huebner, T. A. (2009). Balanced assessment. *Educational Leadership, 67*(3), 85–87.

Jacobs, H. H. (1997). *Mapping the big picture: Integrating curriculum and assessment K–12.* Alexandria, VA: Association for Supervision and Curriculum Development.

Leahy, S., Lyon, C., Thompson, M., & Wiliam, D. (2005). Classroom assessment: Minute by minute, day by day. *Educational Leadership*, *63*(3), 18–24.

Lougy, R., DeRuvo, S., & Rosenthal, D. (2007). *Teaching young children with ADHD: Successful strategies and practical interactions for preK–3*. Thousand Oaks, CA: Corwin Press.

Mager, R. (1962). *Preparing instructional objectives*. Palo Alto, CA: Fearon.

Marshall, K. (2008). Interim assessments: A user's guide. *Phi Delta Kappan*, *90*(1), 64–68.

Marzano, R. J. (2006). *Classroom assessment and grading that work*. Alexandria, VA: Association for Supervision and Curriculum Development.

Marzano, R. J. (2009). *Designing and teaching learning goals and objectives*. Bloomington, IN: Marzano Research Laboratory.

Marzano, R. J. (2010). *Formative assessment and standards-based grading*. Bloomington, IN: Marzano Research Laboratory.

Marzano, R. J., & Kendall, J. S. (1996). *A comprehensive guide to designing standards-based districts, schools, and classrooms*. Alexandria, VA: Association for Supervision and Curriculum Development.

McKinsey & Company. (2009, April). *The educational impact of the achievement gap in America's schools*. Accessed at www.mckinsey.com/App_Media/Images/Page_Images/Offices/SocialSector/PDF/achievement_gap_report.pdf on November 6, 2009.

McNeil, M. (2009, August 12). Rich prize, restrictive guidelines: Criteria would set high bar for "race to the top" eligibility. *Education Week*, pp. 1–23.

Moody, M. S., & Stricker, J. M. (2009). *Strategic design for student achievement*. New York: Teachers College Press.

National Center for Education Statistics. (2009). *Special analysis 2009: International assessments*. Accessed at http://nces.ed.gov/programs/coe/2009/analysis on October 2, 2009.

National Commission on Excellence in Education. (1983). *A nation at risk: The imperative for educational reform*. Washington, DC: U.S. Department of Education.

Nitko, A. J. (2004). *Educational assessment of students* (4th ed.). Upper Saddle River, NJ: Prentice Hall.

O'Connor, K. (2007a). The last frontier: Tackling the grading dilemma. In D. Reeves (Ed.), *Ahead of the curve: The power of assessment to transform teaching and learning* (pp. 126–145). Bloomington, IN: Solution Tree Press.

O'Connor, K. (2007b). *A repair kit for grading: 15 fixes for broken grades*. Portland, OR: Educational Testing Service.

O'Connor, K. (2009). *How to grade for learning, K–12* (3rd ed.). Thousand Oaks, CA: Corwin Press.

Pogrow, S. (2009). Teaching content outrageously: Instruction in the era of on-demand entertainment. *Phi Delta Kappan*, *90*(5), 379–383.

Popham, W. J. (1999). *Classroom assessment: What teachers need to know* (2nd ed.). Boston: Allyn & Bacon.

Popham, W. J. (2006). *Assessment for educational leaders*. Boston: Allyn & Bacon.

Popham, W. J. (2008). *Transformative assessment*. Alexandria, VA: Association for Supervision and Curriculum Development.

Rebora, A. (2008). Making a difference: An interview with Carol Ann Tomlinson. *Teacher Magazine*, *2*(1), 26, 28–31.

Reeves, D. B. (2003). *Making standards work: How to implement standards-based assessments in the classroom, school, and district* (3rd ed.). Englewood, CO: Advanced Learning Press.

Reeves, D. B. (2004, December). The case against the zero. *Phi Delta Kappan, 86*(4), 324–325.

Reeves, D. B. (2006). *The learning leader: How to focus school improvement for better results.* Alexandria, VA: Association for Supervision and Curriculum Development.

Reeves, D. B. (2009). *Leading change in your school: How to conquer myths, build commitment, and get results.* Alexandria, VA: Association for Supervision and Curriculum Development.

Roy, P. (2009, March). Focus on NSDC's standards: Don't wait to find time—create it. *The Learning Principal, 4*(6), 3.

Scherer, M. (2001). How and why standards can improve student achievement: A conversation with Robert J. Marzano. *Educational Leadership, 59*(1), 14–15.

Schmoker, M. (2006). *Results now: How we can achieve unprecedented improvements in teaching and learning.* Alexandria, VA: Association for Supervision and Curriculum Development.

Schmoker, M. (2009). What money can't buy: Powerful, overlooked opportunities for learning. *Phi Delta Kappan, 90*(7), 524–527.

Scriven, M. (1967). The methodology of evaluation. In R. W. Tyler, R. M. Gagne, & M. Scriven (Eds.), *Perspectives of curriculum evaluation, Vol. 1* (pp. 39–83). Chicago: Rand McNally.

Shores, C. (2009). *A comprehensive RTI model: Integrating behavioral and academic interventions.* Thousand Oaks, CA: Corwin Press.

Shulman, L. (1988). A union of insufficiencies: Strategies for teacher assessment in a period of reform. *Educational Leadership, 46*(3), 36–41.

Solomon, P. G. (1998). The curriculum bridge: From standards to actual classroom practice. Thousand Oaks, CA: Corwin Press.

Solomon, P. G. (2002). *The assessment bridge: Positive ways to link tests to learning, standards, and curriculum improvement.* Thousand Oaks, CA: Corwin Press.

Sternberg, R. J. (1985). *Beyond IQ: A triarchic theory of human intelligence.* New York: Cambridge University Press.

Sternberg, R. J. (1988). *The triarchic mind: A new theory of human intelligence.* New York: Viking.

Sternberg, R. J. (2007/2008, December/January). Assessing what matters. *Educational Leadership, 65*(4), 20–26.

Sternberg, R. J., & Williams, W. M. (1996). *How to develop student creativity.* Alexandria, VA: Association for Supervision and Curriculum Development.

Stiggins, R. J., Arter, J. A., Chappuis, J., & Chappuis, S. (2004). *Classroom assessment for student learning: Doing it right—using it well.* Portland, OR: ETS Assessment Training Institute.

Stiggins, R., & DuFour, R. (2009). Maximizing the power of formative assessments. *Phi Delta Kappan, 90*(9), 640–644.

Tirozzi, G. N. (2009, February 25). Principals' perspective: The case for national standards. *Education Week*, p. 23.

Tomlinson, C. A., & Eidson, C. C. (2003). *Differentiation in practice: A resource guide for differentiating curriculum, grades 5–9.* Alexandria, VA: Association for Supervision and Curriculum Development.

United States Department of Education. (2009). *Race to the Top fund: Notice of proposed priorities.* Accessed at www.ed.gov/legislation/FedRegister/proprule/2009-3/072909d.html on November 10, 2009.

Vagle, N. M. (2009). Inspiring and requiring action. In T. Guskey (Ed.), *The teacher as assessment leader* (pp. 203–225). Bloomington, IN: Solution Tree Press.

Vatterott, C. (2009). *Rethinking homework: Best practices that support diverse needs.* Alexandria, VA: Association for Supervision and Curriculum Development.

Vygotsky, L. (1978). *Mind in society.* Cambridge, MA: Harvard University Press.

Wiliam, D. (2007). Content then process: Teacher learning communities in the service of formative assessment. In D. Reeves (Ed.), *Ahead of the curve: The power of assessment to transform teaching and learning* (pp. 183–204). Bloomington, IN: Solution Tree Press.

Young, A. (2009). Using common assessments in uncommon courses. In T. Guskey (Ed.), *The teacher as assessment leader* (pp. 135–153). Bloomington, IN: Solution Tree Press.

Index

V

Vagle, N. M., 104
Vatterott, C., 22, 57
Venn diagram, 82, 131, 133, 134
vertical team, 17
Viegut, D., 23, 24, 30
visual learner, 121
vocabulary logs
    mathematics, 124–127
    science, 123–124

W

weighted rubric, 101–102
Wiliam, D., 21, 43, 139
Williams, W. M., 57
wraparound strategy, 137–139
    stems, 138

Y

Young, A., 27

Ahead of the Curve: The Power of Assessment to Transform Teaching and Learning
Edited by Douglas Reeves

Get the anthology that offers the ideas and recommendations of many of the world's leaders in assessment. Various perspectives of effective assessment design and implementation culminate in a call for redirecting assessment to improve student achievement and inform instruction. **BKF232**

The Teacher as Assessment Leader
Edited by Thomas R. Guskey

Meaningful examples, expert research, and real-life experiences illustrate the capacity and responsibility every educator has to ignite positive change. Packed with practical strategies for designing, analyzing, and using assessments, this book shows how to turn best practices into usable solutions. **BKF345**

Formative Assessment & Standards-Based Grading
Robert J. Marzano

Learn everything you need to know to implement an integrated system of assessment and grading. Robert Marzano explains how to design, interpret, and systematically use three different types of formative assessments and how to track student progress and assign meaningful grades. **BKL003**

40 Reading Intervention Strategies for K–6 Students
Research-Based Support for RTI
Elaine K. McEwan-Adkins

This well-rounded collection of reading intervention strategies, teacher-friendly lesson plans, and adaptable miniroutines will support and inform your RTI efforts. Many of the strategies motivate all students as well as scaffold struggling readers. Increase effectiveness by using the interventions across grade-level teams or schoolwide. **BKF270**

Power Tools for Adolescent Literacy: Strategies for Learning
Jan Rozzelle and Carol Scearce

Power Tools for Adolescent Literacy integrates key strategies from Robert Marzano's meta-analysis, research from top literacy experts, and the proven intervention practices of professional learning communities in a comprehensive collection of best practices and powerful literacy tools for middle-school teachers. **BKF261**

Enriched Learning Projects: A Practical Pathway to 21ˢᵗ Century Skills
James Bellanca
Foreword by Bob Pearlman

Translate standards-based content into enriched learning projects that build 21st century skills. A valuable tool for teachers, this book helps develop critical thinking and creative skills, highlights useful e-tools, and presents a variety of research-based instructional strategies. **BKF296**

Solution Tree | Press
a division of

Solution Tree

Visit solution-tree.com or call 800.733.6786 to order.